D0682989

Dreams and Reflections
## COLLECTION

# SCHOOL OF DESIRES

Reflections 1

**ALSO BY SYLVIE GENDREAU**
Published by Céra

### *City of Intelligences*
Rumors of the Future Collection — Essay

### *School of Desires*
#### *Reflections 2*
Dreams and Reflections Collection
2004

© CÉRA, MONTREAL, 2004
Reflections 1 & 2 — ISBN 2-921788-07-1
Reflections 1 only — ISBN 2-921788-08-X
Dépôt légal — National Library of Quebec, 2004
Dépôt légal — National Library of Canada, 2004

# SYLVIE GENDREAU

Photographs and Drawings
Pierre Guité

# SCHOOL OF DESIRES

Reflections 1

Translated by Robert Majzels and Erin Mouré

Les éditions Céra

To the memory of my parents

Don't tell me everything.

Let me imagine

what follows.

Let me guess

what lies behind

those closed doors.

**THE DESIRE FOR THE DESIRE**

Solitary pleasures,
murmurs
and silence…

"Between the way we want to live and
the agitation without transcendence that marks most of our days,
there is a fissure open in the soul which keeps people from happiness,
as an exile is kept from his native land."[1]

Ernesto Sabato

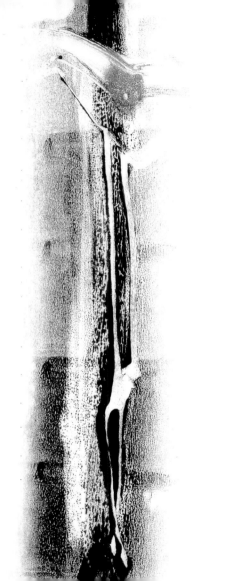

0

I started this book in Venice, on a small island, away from the crowds, with the feeling that I was tiptoeing into a place the world had long forgotten, and knowing my time there was limited. I had only a very few days to take advantage of the quiet before the place would be overrun. I had but five blank pages in my agenda. The perfect opportunity.

The winter of 2002 was drawing to a close. The staff was busy putting the finishing touches on the annual cleanup, preparing for the arrival of the tourists and the grand reopening of the hotel. I had reserved a room in the small Pallazio, the only hotel open this early. From there I could see across the lagoon to the Piazza San Marco and the dome of the Basilica.

I'd left Paris on a whim. A seminar on leadership that I was to facilitate for a group of managers from a large French company had been postponed at the last minute, leaving me a few free days with no appointments. I was tired, I needed to get away, and my sweetheart had suggested Venice; these were the circumstances under which I'd arrived in the city at that precise moment of my life.

My life. For a long time, it had seemed to me like a whirlwind, because of my great desire to change things. At the first glimpse of the slightest hope, I would throw myself full tilt into some project or other. On top of that, I had trouble saying no to any kind of request. No wonder my free time had become such a rare commodity.

Much of the time, I'd been in a mad rush, caught up in a perpetual crisis. I had the feeling that I was mostly occupied with mundane tasks rather than doing what really interested me. There were days when I simply wasn't living the life I aspired to. On other days, I'd be convinced that it wasn't too late to break free, and I made the decisions that would help me take my fate back into my own hands, or at least have the illusion I was doing so.

In his *Book of Disquiet*, Fernando Pessoa describes life as "an experimental journey, undertaken involuntarily. It is a journey of the spirit through the material world and, since it is the spirit that travels, it is in the spirit that it is experienced. That is why there exist contemplative souls who have lived more intensely, more widely, more tumultuously than others who have lived their lives purely externally. The end result is what matters. What one felt was what one experienced. One retires to bed as wearily from having dreamed as from having done hard physical labor. One never lives so intensely as when one has been thinking hard."[2]

To think. Sometimes it seems as though that's all I do. I suppose I think too much. Because I'm such a dreamer, I sometimes feel that I'm imagining my life instead of living it; other times, I fear I'm losing my dreams in life's daily grind.

I've always had trouble accepting the dark moments in my life. I don't like unhappy endings. I'd prefer to leave a trace of beauty in my wake.

I can't bear the notion that some people are fated to suffer.

Sometimes I imagine I'm an African. How does a woman in the Congo who has been raped, and her children taken from her before the age of sixteen to become soldiers, find the strength to go on? How does she keep going, knowing that in the last five years close to five million of her neighbors have died, and that the genocide continues with no end in sight?

On such difficult days, I ask myself why such destinies exist. I'm not African, nor do I live in a country that oppresses women; I'm Canadian, a free woman with plenty of opportunities; and yet I also share a common destiny with all those other women.

What am I doing with this precious gift of freedom? Am I living it fully as a woman, in my innermost being, or am I letting myself drift off course without reacting?

Looking back, I can't complain. With every desire, every experience, I've enriched my life. I've had many dreams, and realized my share of them. Even in times of sadness, I always have a pocketful of desires to draw from. My disappointments may bring me down, but my ideals pick me right back up and lift me even higher.

Saverio Tomasella believes that "humans are conceived as beings, free in their existence, responsible for what they do with their lives and to humanity in general, as well as to each individual around them, regardless of race, religion, philosophy, or the choices they make in life…"[3]

That goes without saying for me, for us, but what about those African women? For them, it seems more difficult. Freedom represents a challenge. An enormous challenge. To be free means the ability to make choices and assume them fully, which is anything but restful. It means a continuous quest. In any case, that's how I see it. And how I live it. To waste such freedom in building a soulless world is a terrible thing.

In my case, to live free means living a little dangerously. On a high wire. At the same time, paradoxically, I always want to make the right choices so that everything turns out all right. I want to feel that I've taken all the necessary risks, that I've answered that knock at the door of desire.

I want to do everything possible so that my freedom isn't wasted, so that it might one day give hope to those who are denied it, and encourage them to struggle for it.

To do everything possible to avoid Pessoa's conclusion: "Unknowingly, I have been a witness to the gradual wasting away of my life, to the slow shipwreck of everything I wanted to be."[4]

Well, there you are, right from the start, I'm admitting one of my greatest fears: my fear of not taking full advantage of my freedom to contribute in some small measure to the beauty of the world. I've ventured this admission because, behind my fear, lies the desire to call upon you to help make a gesture of beauty so that together we might create the *School of Desires.*

I'd love to enroll in a *School of Desires*,
to banish the fears that paralyze us.

This tandem of fear-desire explains why I alternate between a life that races forward, fuelled by passion, and a life that slows down as I realize that my passion has turned into something far less compelling: mere agitation. It might help me earn my living, but isn't really what I want to do. And it's at precisely those moments that I must listen to my heart and find the courage to change my life, to risk it all. Once again. **Because isn't life, fully lived, really a continual series of new beginnings?**

Of course, I believe in fate, but I also believe we make choices that determine which road we take; we open doors that make it possible for us to build something based on our ideals, to translate our dreams into reality. Hermann Hesse wrote: "Whether we paint or write poetry, or whether we simply aspire to create ourselves, invent ourselves, thus taking pleasure in our creative power, we all find ourselves constantly confronting these inevitable disruptions."[5]

It's part of human fate, as Marguerite Yourcenar says, to struggle between what we want to be, what we believe we are, and what we will become.

Like most people, when I find myself swept up in a whirl of activity and besieged by the overload that results, I have a hard time finding calm, and seeing clearly once more in order to make the right decisions, or even hear that knock at the door of desire.

That day, riding through Paris in a taxi on my way to Charles de Gaulle airport, I was in exactly that beleaguered state. I had grave doubts that just another airplane ride — especially when the stay was going to be so short — would be enough to refocus my life and desires.

To my surprise, as soon as I arrived in Venice, I suddenly felt calm. Looking at the sea and sky flowing into each other in shades of turquoise, my ridiculous little troubles seemed to dissolve into the milky aquarelle. My telephone could go right on ringing, my body, and my spirit even more so, were not in the same zone as the tinny voices calling from Montreal and Paris.

Stendhal was right when he said that a person goes to Italy, not to discover it, but to be happy there. Speeding along in the taxi, my face whipped by cool air and sea spray, it never occurred to me to go inside.

The calming effect was instantaneous and left me momentarily stunned. It was as if someone had hurtled me into the sky, giving me a new perspective on my life. A photograph taken from above. A completely different view. Larger. More expansive.

I opened my eyes wide and gazed out at the surrounding beauty as though it were the last time I would see it. In the past, I would have said: "It's beautiful here; I'll be back."

On that Tuesday, March 19, 2002, Venice was so beautiful that I thought: now I can die. Not that I wanted to die, but I felt so peaceful, so satisfied, that I would have been content to end it all right there, at that moment.

It was something I had not felt in such a long time. I was the kind of person always in a hurry — not to say harried — because I always felt I hadn't accomplished enough.

I feared the years were passing too quickly for someone who hoped to achieve something in this life. Now, here I was, abandoning myself to this mysterious condition, this strange feeling of well-being and complete release.

The sun had become warm enough to turn the lawns green. I sat on a bench with a book — either in the garden under a tree, where I could smell the fresh grass and hear the birds celebrate the first days of spring, or near the lagoon with its quiet murmuring water. I breathed gently. I was content.

It took this brief Venetian interlude, this astonishing moment of grace in my otherwise agitated life, to catch my breath and rekindle my desire.

## The Desire for the Desire

In my room, the moon was my only companion. It was so close and full, it drew me into an intimate dialogue. From my reading chair to my desk, it followed my every move. I found myself whispering my innermost thoughts and feelings to it. Which road should I take? Wasn't it time I rethink my desires? Alone, quiet and serene, I floated in a state of total happiness, as though a breath of fresh air had brought my neglected dreams back to life. I felt that, after a rest, I could once again don my seven-league boots and bring those dreams to fruition.

At that point, I was still participating in conference calls with managers and politicians, but I had a sense of being much farther away than they imagined. Life has its share of sudden collapses, shocks, rejections, but even mundane disappointments can build up to the point where you lose even the will to desire. That's what had happened to me.

By the time my plane landed in the small Venice airport, I was burnt out. The effects of continual stress were etched on my face, along with the disappointment of having let myself slip into a way of life that was drawing me away from any chance at true happiness. I was upset that I'd let myself be dragged down by a society that cared little for others and had no respect for nature. A society of appearances, full of misleading discourses; a society based on performance and false productivity. I had the unpleasant feeling of having sold out to it — as a consultant to senior management — and sometimes even of being an instrument of its manipulations. I felt an inner dissatisfaction fed by simmering rage at the lack of integrity, the power games, the will to conquest and the insatiable thirst for huge profits that benefit a very few. Not to mention those who, once in power, refuse to share the spotlight.

I blamed those in power for their lack of vision and refusal to share, but I was more disappointed by the apathy of the rest of us. Are we going to let human values be replaced by financial ones? Are we going to allow a very small group of executives decide what's best for the entire planet? How much longer are we going to abandon so many women and children?

The historian and feminist Elisabeth Badinter offers us some insight. She says that we live in a society that treats victims like heroes. We are called to join so many causes that I, for one, find my heart begins to harden. Marketing campaigns against abuse and exploitation end up abusing me. I feel manipulated.

I want real heroes, and I want to be sure we are helping the real victims, those who may not even have the strength to complain. And when I say helping them, I mean encouraging them to realize their own dreams, to build their own lives and nations, to become autonomous. It does not mean making them dependent on us; it means encouraging them to use their own wings to fly. That's what groups like those of Father Ceyrac and Sister Emmanuelle have so admirably done in France. They are my kind of heroes; people who never tire of demonstrating that love conquers all.

On the other hand, victims who complain constantly, but refuse to make the effort to improve their lot leave me indifferent. They are a sign to me that our society is in trouble. You have to admit that more and more victims and fewer heroes does not a healthy society make. The myth of the hero is not dead, but these days, heroes are, more often than not, the creations of mass marketing campaigns. We live in a world of appearances, where the desire for fame seems to dominate all else.

Take for example top-level athletes: we don't care if they drug themselves to death before they reach thirty, so long as they provide a good show. And woe to anyone who dares express a contrary opinion. No one is allowed to cast a shadow on the spectacle.

The same holds true in so many fields. We are manipulated, for the most part with our consent. We participate in this grand simulacrum that has become the new reality. To me, people seem blocked. Politicians, employers and union leaders have all cut themselves off in their struggles for power. Huge structures remain paralyzed because we are caught up in our fixed ideas, each side entrenched in our positions. What can shake us out of such torpor?

I developed a collective intelligence approach (presented in chapter four and in greater detail in *City of Intelligences*), which yields excellent results when all participants agree to share power. But as soon as one group, whether employers or unions, starts to think and decide for the others, all is lost. Because collective intelligence, as the name implies, means allowing each person to exercise their intelligence and truly contribute to building the whole, on the basis of unifying values such as integrity, respect, dignity, cooperation — values from another age, Ernesto Sabato would say.

A collective intelligence approach encourages all individuals to develop their intelligence to the best of their abilities, and to be less easily manipulated. It is a disturbing approach for those who do not want to share power.

My anger and lassitude stemmed from no longer knowing what role to play in this society. My words and actions had been drained of any meaning, and I felt like Don Quixote who, barely returned home from his journey, found everything on the road behind him had already turned to dust. I had taken brief pleasure from time to time, in a successful conference or seminar, but the net result struck me as far too meager.

Faced with disappointments, I'd lost my desires and my energy. I moved liked a robot, wondering if I was being overly critical, or if my analysis of the planet's future had some basis in truth. Was I becoming more lucid, but also more frustrated, and therefore less able to act? To cast a dark pessimistic gaze on the world was no solution either. That much I knew.

Engulfed in Venice's magic, its mists, murmurs and silence, I felt deeply at peace. I felt the mystery of this place, the possibility of imagining a thousand and one worlds. And it had happened so suddenly. As though, combined with my solitude and soul-searching, Venice had alchemical powers.

It was already time to go. Standing in the vaporetto, I left my small island retreat to join a young French friend named Mathieu and his cousin Marco, a Florentine architect. They had driven all morning from a small Italian village to see me. We had agreed to meet in front of St. Mark's Basilica. They were a splendid sight: smiling, barely a care in the world, two young men, free, their eyes ablaze with dreams and ideals.

I was a little sad to leave this place that had so enchanted me. Marco's French and my Italian being less than adequate, Mathieu provided his somewhat free translations all through lunch. Thanks to the two of them, my stay ended in peals of laughter.

I like these young idealists. With them and for their sake, I could once again believe it is not too late to dream and change the world. That midday in Venice, we were already three.

Before I'd left Paris, my friend Sylvie had quoted Saint Francis of Assisi to me: "Do not merely attempt to change the world; rather change worlds." Wise advice, I thought.

Whenever this world seems too depressing, I remind myself that we can always invent new ones. In the end, that may be the best way to help those now struggling in the most sordid trenches. We ought to invent worlds that inspire them to go on and create even more beautiful ones. "We demonize what we should reinterpret and use as material for a better dream. It's by inventing a new world that we can resist…," writes Alessandro Baricco in his essay *Next*. Speaking of globalization, he adds: "It's a dull dream, because it is the product of the imagination of CEOs and bankers. In a sense, our task is to begin to dream this dream in their place, and then to achieve it. It's a question of imagination, tenacity and anger. Perhaps this is the task before us."[6]

Dreaming is a resource within everyone's grasp, regardless of race, religion, nationality. A dream is our primary source of power, and desire gives us the strength to realize it.

This book of my personal reflections is simply a proposal to create a *School of Desires* and to start dreaming a new world together. I don't believe we should exclude anyone, neither bankers nor CEOs; however, they too must agree to share their power, and invite us all to participate intelligently in building the whole. I offer this proposal to my friends and to all those who, like me, desire something new.

In 1998, I wrote *City of Intelligences* to invite you all to build that city, through an approach I call collective intelligence. I'm still surprised by how many readers stumbled upon this work along their way, and continue to write me about their own experiences, which read like fables of desire. These messages coming to me from so many different places have pushed me to dream.

I threw a message in a bottle into the sea and replies came from everywhere. It made me want to continue this dialogue. Almost six years later, I'm returning from my wanderings with the desire to share my conclusions, disappointments and hopes.

In his *Invisible Cities*, Italo Calvino writes, "With cities, it is as with dreams: everything imaginable can be dreamed, but even the most unexpected is a rebus that conceals a desire or, its reverse, a fear. Cities, like dreams, are made of desires and fears, even if the thread of their discourse is secret, their rules are absurd, their perspectives deceitful, and everything conceals something else."[7] That's what I learned in the course of my own journeys. I want to give you an intimate and personal report of those journeys. Your response to my first call was so generous that you made me want to write again. And those Venetian canals were so inviting. And the bottles so beautiful, that I could not resist sending you another. *Prego!*

Venice, March 2002.

A DISARMING IDEA OF BEAUTY

« Beauty will save the world. »

Dostoevski

1

I'd barely landed at Charles de Gaulle airport and turned on my cell phone when a client called. He seemed surprised by all my comings and goings. He must have thought I was incapable of sitting still. My clients travel mainly out of necessity or to visit family, but rarely to relax. Their time is too precious to waste it gazing for hours at the moon over the lagoon.

Not that I'm complaining. Why would I? I'm privileged. My work and my clients allow me a great deal of autonomy. Without them, my Venetian escapade wouldn't have been possible, at least not in the same conditions. I recognize this and I'm grateful to them. The more life is full, the more we appreciate the chance to relax.

By the time I was done with my phone call, my bags were the only ones left on the carrousel. Outside, waiting for a taxi, I breathed in the spring air that blew softly over Paris that evening.

I had a sudden urge to call my sweetheart in Montreal to tell him I loved him, and to thank him for having encouraged me to spend those few days in Venice. Everything seemed lighter, easier. It was a lesson I would do well to remember: to take such quiet breaks in my life more often. Silence is never far from dreaming. At least as far as I'm concerned. I only have to be quiet for a bit and my imagination awakens. "It doesn't matter what we dream; what we dream is true," Pessoa wrote. I agree.

In my suitcase, I'd brought back the scraps and jottings of the dream that had started to take form in Venice. Before leaving Montreal, I'd worked on a talk I was to give in five months to the annual general meeting of the School Boards of Quebec. I'd arranged to meet young people and teachers, and have them dream up their vision of the ideal school. We filmed them as they did so. I wanted to share their comments with others and, more importantly, to include them in dreaming the school of the future.

To my great surprise, I found that, after nine years in the school system, young people were all out of desires. Of course, we have to take into account that they are in mid-adolescence, a difficult time of life. But that alone could not explain the problem.

Several of their comments stayed with me, and I'll return to these later, but one in particular that struck me concerned the beauty of their surroundings. I was in one of Quebec's most beautiful schools, yet several students commented on the sameness of the classrooms, the dull colors of the walls, and the concrete schoolyard, void of trees or grass.

Several complained that they rarely went out on school field trips. They claimed they could learn more outside the school than in it.

Others had no desire to dream at all, because they no longer felt concerned about the school. For them, high school would soon be a distant memory. They were simply not interested in rethinking the institution for the benefit of those who would follow.

Some felt that the teachers weren't teaching them to think for themselves. Others seemed exhausted just at the thought of thinking.

I was taken aback; in fact, I was stunned. As the editors and I screened the video footage, we were depressed. These young people were the future, and they seemed a thousand miles from their desires.

For many of them, their greatest wish was to become a film, music or sports star. Some of the young women looked more like blond bombshells than young students. They were a microcosm of our society, drugged by the advertising images of pop culture divas.

Many of them were pessimistic about the possibilities of a better world, and saw no way that they could do anything to change it. It wasn't even worth trying, since there was no hope.

But in the more gifted classes, students did dream of building a more humane world. The special attention they were given, and the international and specialized courses at their disposal, had borne fruit. But it was a drop in the ocean. Only one class among so many others.

I can still see myself on that cold winter day, slightly shocked, in front of a class of young people in their last year of high school. I couldn't resign myself to the sight of so many blank stares and amorphous gestures. It was heart-wrenching. I felt like shouting Rilke's advice to a young poet: "Do you not see that everything that takes place is ever and again a beginning, since beginning in itself is always of such beauty?"[1]

Were we, the older generation, so blasé that young people were depressed even before beginning their adult lives? What had we done? Had too many of us painted a bleak picture of the world and communicated it to the next generation?

But above all, what could we do to help them want to desire, to invent and to build? To give them the desire to live?

Having lived through one of history's bloodiest centuries, Jean D'Ormesson recalls that being happy was once rather frowned upon. "I took up a relatively unpopular position on the chessboard, one others tended to avoid. It was in bad form. Inappropriate," he writes. "Beside the horrors that had never stopped raining down, one after the other, there were also roses, moments of the day embroidered in silk thread, irascible old folks who left behind tender memories, children to love, wonderful things to read, to see, to hear, excellent things to eat and drink… I was more inclined to laughter and saying yes than to tears and saying no. I tended more to praise and wonderment than to derision and blame. I was an exception. What luck!"[2]

Those who seek beauty will find it.

After several weeks thinking about those young people's lack of desire – caused by our own cynicism – it was in Venice that I at last had the idea of a *School of Desires*.

Imagine creating something that brings us pleasure today, and continues to bring pleasure decades later. Could those who built Venice have imagined that one day it would be so magical, not because of its grandeur and riches, but thanks to its poetry and the dreams it engenders.

If people were able to build a place as magical and poetic as Venice, it seems to me that we in turn can build the *School of Desires*. A school with the sky for a roof, the trees and mountains for walls. A school that would help us to see the beauties of this world and teach us to better protect them. A school in the tradition of Socrates that would teach us to think for ourselves.

When I read the travel diaries of people writing in the early twentieth century, I regret that we will never enjoy the places they describe, because the beauty of those places has been destroyed.

We develop, build and overpopulate at such a rate that virgin lands and beautiful cities have become rare. The speed with which we are capable of eradicating beauty on this earth, whether in times of war or peace, is mind-boggling.

The Earth is only ours on loan. Each of our actions can result in either dire consequences or beauty. Consider creators: even though they are really doing it to please themselves their acts leave behind marvelous traces in the world.

Returning from a trip to Italy in 1907, Herman Hesse wrote: "I thought again of San Miniato, the cupola and tower of the Domo of Florence, and of what had again attracted me to these masterpieces. Why had they made me happy? Because, seeing them, I felt that the work and passion of a man are not in vain, that beyond the oppressive solitude of each of our lives, there exists a good shared by all, desirable and marvelous. In each era, hundreds of people have suffered and worked alone so that this consoling good might take shape. What artists and their students accomplished with devotion and perseverance several hundred years ago still provoke a thousand beautiful thoughts in us today. So it is that to continue to work despite feeling alone and impotent, to put all our strength into what we do, does not seem hopeless to us. It was exactly that sort of consolation I had sought, and nothing more." He continues: "I had always known that this common good existed, but it is not a bad thing to rediscover what we know; once more we have direct experience of the presence of the past, the proximity of times long gone, the permanence of the beautiful. Each time it awakens in us a feeling of surprise and joy. Michelangelo and Fra Angelico were certainly not thinking of me, nor of anyone else for that matter, as they worked. They created for themselves, each thinking only of himself, which caused them some unhappiness; they had to struggle bitterly against discouragement and exhaustion. Both of them were entirely dissatisfied with the products of their labor. Ghirlandaio dreamt of more lively paintings, Michelangelo of more imposing buildings and monuments. Today all that remains of their work is what has escaped destruction, and yet it seems to us that, in spite of everything, their efforts were not in vain, and this gives us courage to continue our own work."[3]

Courage – that's what we need to create our *School of Desires*. A century has gone by, but Hermann Hesse's reflections still ring true. The effort is not in vain and, although we do it primarily for ourselves, our efforts can also bring happiness to others. To share snatches of beauty, to remember beautiful things, to invent and tell new stories for the children of our children: this is the crazy challenge I propose we accept together.

In his book, *Resistance*, Ernesto Sabato argues that "we can't keep reading our children tales of the little red hen and her chicks, while we inflict the worst sorts of torture on these same animals."[4]

We have to reinvent ourselves so we can create new stories that we can read without shame to our children. Is it utopian to think we might live out our dreams? I hope not.

Nine PM. The cab was advancing at a snail's pace. Two hours stuck in bumper-to-bumper traffic on a Friday evening in Paris will make anyone impatient. There was some sort of demonstration near my apartment. I admire those who keep their calm driving in this city. I get agitated even as a passenger; I can't imagine how I would act if I were behind the wheel.

The taxi driver, a young Senegalese man, was telling me how happy he and his family were to be living in France. He'd had a difficult life, which made him that much more grateful.

I was moved by his optimism and courage. Listening to him, I recalled the words of Hermann Hesse, that the true character of a man is revealed in crisis. I've met many Africans who maintain this lightness of being despite the difficulties they have faced.

The taxi stopped in front of my home on the rue d'Artois, in the 8th arrondissement. As the evening wears on, my neighborhood turns into an outdoor nightclub. The nearby hotels, bars and the Champs-Elysées all contribute to the nightly racket. It was a fine place for going out, but not so good for sleeping. After my silent retreat, the contrast was striking.

I opened my windows, which looked out over the rooftops of Paris. I adore such changes of surroundings. I love coming home. I like to leave in order to return. I love to rediscover the beauty of a place. My gaze takes in everything; it all seems sharper, brighter. I set down my suitcase and went out again to buy food.

I'm always glad to return to this city I adore. My best friends are here. But that evening everything felt different. I'd drunk the magic potion of Venice. I wondered how many days I'd be under its influence.

In Paris my life was always intense. I even walked fast or, rather, I raced. Whereas in Venice, I'd felt almost immobile, suspended between earth and sky. It was a feeling I enjoyed.

In order to appreciate a landscape or the clouds, shouldn't a person be able to meditate with them?

Hoping with all my heart that my trip to Venice would not be in vain, I was determined to slow down whenever beauty crossed my path.

The *School of Desires* of which I dream is a struggle for beauty. Isn't it worth fighting to preserve a poetic view of the world?

In the words of Marguerite Yourcenar, one must stubbornly maintain the ability to see in the dark.

That night I felt a crazy desire to light up the darkness, to rake sparks of poetry from the embers. I wanted to find inspiration in everything I saw and heard. To gorge myself on desires. It was up to me to see, or rather to relearn to see. Up to me to let myself be surprised by the beauty of things.

To see. Some days it's easier than others. Each time I come back to Paris, for example, it's as though — in passing from a street corner into a square, across a bridge and past a monument — I forget how the beauty of the city shimmers and teaches me elegance. Beauty, imagined and built by men and women: legions of hearts at work, hands attending to their task, ingenious minds designing a masterpiece, then another, and another. These splendid structures multiply before my eyes to create an even greater beauty: the harmony of the whole. One building's façade draws attention to the excellence of another, a garden extends the architecture of a palace, a play of lighting adds mystery to the square.

In the symphony of images, in their complimentary gestures, it's the alchemy that impresses me most. Alchemy between the creators' inspired ideas, and the artisans attaining the summit of their art by making real the ambitious dreams of geniuses.

Individual intelligences come together, single drops of perspiration gradually accumulate into a great expanse of water. There's a tacit understanding that each will do his best; without this collective intelligence nothing would be possible.

Each time a top fashion designer announces that it is closing down, I think of those small hands, working with such precision to incarnate a creator's dream on a body in motion. Will such seamstresses continue to exist in a world that values artisans so little? I think of the French launderers who wash the finest, most delicate textiles without damaging them. They work hand in hand to create beauty and then to protect it, to maintain it in its original condition.

My proposal: Beauty as a political act.

Imagine a plot to make everything beautiful: the clothes we wear, the places where we walk, the sculptures we admire. That's how I see Paris when its streets have been deserted by the crowds of stressed people, when my eyes take the time to look and sweep gently over my surroundings.

As I strolled along, I was thinking about the cleaners on rue d'Artois, owned by a couple who are passionate about their craft. Their expertise is such that the most demanding clients are forever thanking them for saving some article of clothing from disaster. Compare that with North American dry-cleaning chains whose industrial processes will destroy your clothing in the blink of an eye. They may return it to you in an hour, but it's as ragged as if you'd worn it for ten years.

Admittedly, it's a very small example, but it illustrates the consequences of our indifference toward artisans. Is their expertise destined to disappear?

When a team of people succeeds in producing quality, we have to ensure that they can earn a living doing it, so that their expertise is not lost. But we do just the opposite. In our era of high speed and performance, the logic of big chains and mega-stores is winning out. It's a logic that demands profits to the detriment of the sort of quality that is only perfected over generations.

Will we wake up too late to do anything but regret the disappearance of a quality workforce, of artisans who put their hearts into their labor, taking satisfaction from a job well done? Meanwhile, chain store profits keep rising, and their customers gradually become sucked into the downward spiral. As soon as profits dip, we are treated to the sudden closing of hundreds of stores and layoffs of thousands of employees. Relying on the big chains and losing the advantages of small business does not necessarily mean job security, nor a higher standard of living for the majority.

My mother used to tell us that we couldn't afford to buy low quality. Today I'm more convinced than ever of the necessity to fight for her standards. I want to believe there will always be a market for quality, if we all demand it together. I want to believe that access to quality will not be limited to the rich. Whenever I can, I encourage small merchants.

Some multinationals shut down factories in countries with strict regulations to establish themselves in places where people can be made to work in any conditions. An excellent report on French television recently showed very young Chinese boys and girls working in a filthy workplace to produce toys for Disney. Toys destined for the amusement of our children are contributing to the suffering of others. How can we tolerate such situations? How can we be the employees of such employers? How can we be consumers who keep these producers alive?

In fact, do we really know what's going on? Aren't we lacking the global overview we really need?

Thankfully, there are journalists who investigate and report the facts; they help us to make the links we might otherwise miss. The difficulty is not just in choosing which information is essential to produce some sort of synthesis from the information overload, but also in separating truth from lies. Some filmmakers help us to see through the slick public relations strategies. Looking back, films like *The Quiet American*, based on Graham Greene's novel, or the documentaries of Michael Moore shed light on certain things that happen, and help us to grasp what might otherwise

elude us. The responsibility then falls on each one of us. Good journalism should be followed up by persistent action. Only such action can give real meaning to contemporary journalism: a multitude of small gestures, of daily commitments.

To make beauty a priority is, to my mind, a political act that opposes acts of war, acts that destroy beauty rather than protecting it.

The war against Iraq is one example, where people the world over felt like going into the streets to say Enough! Most people agreed that Iraq had to be disarmed and the Iraqis supported in their struggle for freedom, but was so much violence and the destruction of historical sites really necessary? Was it even effective?

The demonstrations for peace throughout the world gave me hope. Even though it may not seem to make much difference, **each act is important.**

With freedom and daring, we could create a place that fosters acts of beauty. The *School of Desires* requires neither walls nor money to exist. It must first be born within our imaginations; the best place to sketch plans and designs. If we persist in designing our dreams, in spite of ourselves, our daily actions will begin to take on new meaning. Because, as Sabato, echoing Pessoa, tells us: "...we can say what we like about dreams, except that they are lies."[5]

I expect very little from governments, but a great deal from us, from our imaginations, our desires, and our actions. "True freedom will not be granted to us by the coming to power of some man or other," Gandhi told us, "but by the power we will have one day to oppose abuses of authority. Individual freedom will see the light of day when we will have given the multitudes the conviction that they have the possibility to control the exercise of power and make themselves respected."[6]

I expect a great deal from us, but first we have to convince ourselves that the beauty of the world is worth waging a constant struggle to preserve. We are creatures of habit who can get used to beauty or to ugliness; but only beauty engenders beauty.

The more I am surrounded by beauty, the more I want to create it. The more I become used to the unacceptable, the more it becomes acceptable. The more I contest it, the less the unacceptable becomes possible. **Each act counts.**

"True beauty is a momentum toward beauty, a fountain at once visible and invisible, that pours forth each instant from the depths of those who are present to it,"[7] says a character in François Cheng's novel *Green Mountain, White Cloud*.

I'd noted in my journal that I was in love with life. In Paris, that Venetian charm was still working. I had managed, in spite of being much busier, to maintain a kind of slowness in my gaze, if not in my pace. The latter had accelerated in tune with others around me in the street. But my spirit resisted any unnecessary agitation. Here I am, praising slowness — I can see the smiles on the faces of those who know me.

A typically Parisian drizzle fell from morning till night. I defy all those who criticize the French for their occasional moodiness to maintain their smile after several days, weeks, and even months of rain. I'm not particularly affected by the weather but, after a few months in Paris, I realized to what extent Montreal is a city of light. It can get very cold there in winter, but there's always a patch of blue sky to brighten your spirits.

I emerged from a meeting with the president of a major French company in one of whose divisions we had been conducting a collective intelligence project during the last year and a half. He was accompanied by a recently named head of that division. The company was in the throes of a major restructuring, a common word in the business world these days.

The changes were so numerous and so swift that neither of them were able to come and meet with those working on the project to discuss its progress. Instead I'd brought them a video of commentary prepared by the teams. I wasn't particularly happy about doing it this way. I did it anyway because I wanted their project to continue, and I wanted the employees to feel that they had the support of the upper management. But we had it backwards. Naturally, the teams would have preferred their president to visit them in person. How can you feel motivated when you feel so unimportant, so unrecognized?

I often sense that managers think that all they have to do is come up with good strategy at the top, and the troops will follow automatically. Everything I've experienced inside companies over the years has convinced me of the opposite. The best results I've witnessed came when teams were given enough leeway to act and had the conviction that they were, in a sense, builders of cathedrals; that is, they had the feeling that each individual was laying his or her stone intelligently, and that their efforts, talent and creativity were being recognized. But some managers are only interested in strategies, treating human concerns as a waste of their time. Reading Italo Calvino, I felt as though history was repeating itself.

**"Marco Polo describes a bridge, stone by stone.**

**'But which is the stone that supports the bridge?' asks Kublai Khan, Emperor of the Tartars.**

'The bridge is not supported by one stone or another,' Marco answers, 'but by the line of the arch they form.'

Kublai Khan remains silent, reflecting. Then he adds: 'Why do you speak to me of the stones? It is only the arch that matters to me."

Polo answers: 'Without stones, there is no arch.'"[8]

In my work on leadership, I am obsessed with sustainability. I prefer to act in a way that gives lasting results. Unfortunately, I sense that, in spite of my efforts, I don't always succeed. That brought me to seriously question myself. Who was I to dare to think I could help others lead? It was a great lesson in humility. Reading Rilke, I found some comfort: "…in the end it is in the most fundamental and crucial of our concerns that we remain unutterably alone. A great deal has to take place for one person to be able to advise or, even more, actually to aid another; a whole constellation of things must come together for that to be successful even once."[9]

A whole constellation of things indeed. These days, in very large companies, there's a constant turnover at the top. Already, our project had been slowed down by a heavy, sluggish structure, many administrative changes and scant resources. Now, they told me that the senior manager overseeing the project was leaving.

That's why I'd asked for this second meeting with the president, having concluded that there wasn't much point in continuing unless the president himself backed the project wholeheartedly. I felt personally responsible for all those who'd believed in it. For them, we had to keep going. The president gave his support, and without the slightest hesitation. I think he truly believed in it. But in the heat of the action, with all the hierarchy, turf wars and power games, I knew it was idealistic to think a process of collective leadership could succeed in a company this huge, with a traditional and bureaucratic structure that gave free rein to those adept at playing the game of amassing more power.

I realized how powerless one person alone could be, regardless of his or her position, if others don't share the same values, or humanist convictions. When the law of profit rules, we think there's no time to nurture people. And yet, people are the very heart of any company.

After my meeting, I went home thinking how hard it is to introduce such an approach into a company, even though it always gives excellent results if we really believe in it and allow it the necessary strategic time. So much time is spent studying figures, graphs and statistics when, to me, the only way to make these go upward is to invest in an approach that let's everyone be responsible, in an atmosphere of mutual respect.

Most managers pay lip service to these principles, but their decisions and actions are rarely consistent with them. The result is just more incoherence.

Admitting this to myself was very difficult, because I'd hoped for so long that things would be different. My projects within companies were like dreams that had lost their luster. Early on, I'd succeeded in realizing several creative projects with open-minded and visionary managers; now I felt this had become less and less possible. It was as though a financial vice had tightened over those in a position to lead, leaving them little room to risk beauty and creativity. Our results had become necessarily less impressive, and the real pleasure of creators and builders had considerably diminished. They'd gone back to carrying out orders, or turned into battle-worn politicians, rather than creators. I had no wish to let myself be drawn into such a drab world. I told myself that if the business world became a mere simulacrum, I would leave it. Life is too short to fight for things that aren't worthwhile.

What worries me is that, with so much of our behavior modeled on business, society as a whole risks becoming increasingly obsessed with profits, and ignoring the human soul. I deplore the fact that so many men and women abdicate, thinking it's the only way they can earn a living. It seems to me that, if no one accepted the situation, it would change. **Each act counts.**

I decided to set my thoughts aside for a few days. I felt like focusing on one thing: beauty. My sweetheart was coming to join me for Easter weekend and — speaking of beauty — we had decided to spend it by the sea in Brittany. Once I reached home, I'd found quiet and an inner calm once again. I thought about how lucky I am to be with a man who lets me do exactly as I please, a man who makes me better and more intelligent. Proof that it's possible to be different.

Paris, March 2002

POWERFUL INFLUENCES

"Often he wished… that he could feel his breath
was like that of the wind over the oceans, that
between the world and him there was
an understanding and an affinity…"[1]

Hermann Hesse

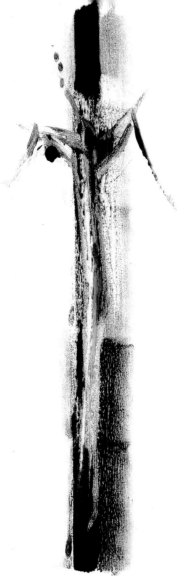

2

Though the taxi had sped through empty streets, the train station was packed. Parisians were abandoning their city to the tourists for a few days. Stepping quickly, we fell in happily with the crowd.

In our excitement, we'd forgotten to punch our tickets before boarding, in order to validate them, as is the rule in France. The ticket collector on the train made a big fuss. You'd have thought we'd forgotten to pay! We tried to explain we were from Quebec and unfamiliar with the rules, but to no avail. Maybe he was feeling particularly fed up that morning, and had decided to take it out on us. For our part, aside from having to restrain our laughter, we weren't seriously upset. But who knows who else he had insulted that day, maybe one of his colleagues, who could have been more adversely affected.

The danger in a society where a small number of people thinks and decides for the whole is that we end up with a population that thinks less and less. To simply execute orders without thinking develops neither individual nor collective intelligence.

The way we manage our companies affects the development of our society. The less consideration we have for people, the less they have for themselves, and for others. Their behavior demonstrates this on a daily basis. Socially, it's a downward spiral.

Geneticists have recently discovered that very little separates the human genetic code from that of the chimpanzee. This knowledge ought to make us a little more humble.

Intelligence is like a muscle. We either develop it or it will atrophy. It's a personal choice, but also a choice that society and companies make. It's difficult to measure the consequences of neglecting intelligence, because we don't easily grasp the bigger picture. Most of the time, we study phenomena in very specialized ways, but we rarely examine how things interact. A panoramic vision and an interdisciplinary approach don't come easily.

Discreetly I studied the ticket collector who was still bawling at us. I wondered how many other people were unhappy enough in their work to become as frustrated and irascible as he was.

If we could measure the negative effect such people have on those around them (in their public and private lives), and the resulting cost in various medicines and therapies, we might be more willing to reexamine our management techniques.

Maybe I ought to learn to be more fatalistic and remind myself that I can't change the way things are. If I were wise, and I'm working at it, I wouldn't let myself be so affected by these social ills. But the moment I let my guard down, and witness some small incident, I immediately return to the eternal question: "What could we do differently?"

## Powerful Influences

In the chill of the early spring, the sight of small train stations and French countryside, enveloped in a sky of mixed sun and cloud, calmed me. In almost no time I'd entered into the vacation spirit. I only had to think of my friends struggling with the cold and snow back in Quebec to appreciate my good fortune. At that time of year, every day stolen from the clutches of winter is a godsend.

I was impatient to see the ocean, and hear the wind. I squeezed my eyes shut to anticipate the pleasure. The sea is a long way from Montreal. It was a joy to think that only a few hours of train travel would bring its splendor within sight. I wondered if Parisians realized how lucky they were.

I read without really retaining anything, falling in and out of sleep, and abandoning myself to the gentle rocking of the train. When I opened my eyes, my sweetheart was there, sitting opposite me, dozing peacefully.

**Our surroundings influence us.** A friend who had traveled to Italy with her sister told me that, as soon as they arrived, they felt an urge to dress more elegantly. They quickly bought accessories to blend in with the Italian crowd. I liked that image. We're all participating in installations, in ephemeral collective works. Along with others, we form life-size paintings in motion. We're inspired by our environment. We act, sometimes consciously, sometimes not, in harmony with the world around us.

I tend to transform myself according to the city I'm in. No sooner do I step into the Parisian crowd than I too become Parisian. My pace quickens. In Rome, after a few moments of impatience, I slow right down. In Venice, I'm bewitched by a kind of poetic mystery.

In Montreal, I feel a certain lightness and joy. We adapt to the rhythm of a city; we are actors constantly playing with others, according to the location in which we find ourselves. We're more important to each other than we realize. Every advertisement, image, behavior and construction nourishes the collective unconscious. **Our acts matter.**

In our creations and actions, we unconsciously reinterpret what we see in the city. I'm a waking dreamer. In my dreams, I sometimes imagine a loose coalition in which we would all look with new eyes at our surroundings; we would learn to see beauty, and then go on to create, build and insist on more beauty.

But what is beauty? Is it a way of seeing, an emotion, a social code, an utopia?

The answer is multiple, which means each person can make up their own. The painter John Constable, whose drawings and landscapes are so magnificent, claimed he'd never seen an ugly thing in his life. I'd love to borrow his eyes.

In Erri De Luca's novel *God's Mountain*, one of the characters says: "… all eyes need tears to see, or else they become like the eyes of fish, which cannot see out of water and dry out, go blind."[2]

Tears and absences both let us see things anew. Each time I come home to Montreal, I rediscover my river at dawn. That spectacular sky never fails to thrill me. And yet, the more I see it, the less I seem to see of it. It's as though my comings and goings allow me to see things with fresh eyes. It's like being reborn and marveling at your first sight of something truly beautiful.

It's true that beauty is highly subjective. What's beautiful to me may not be beautiful to you. What inspires me may not necessarily inspire you. "Beauty is certainly the site of intercultural controversy," Michel Sauquet says in the preface to the essay on beauty, "and not only between geographically distant cultures, but also among our own circles of acquaintance".[3]

To think about beauty, to be sensitive to it, is already a source of hope. Our circles of acquaintances can also become circles of taste. Nostalgia aside, I sometimes fear that beauty and the aesthetic are no longer important values in our contemporary societies, that they've been replaced by commercial values in the interest of quick profits.

What other conclusion can I come to when I see cities painted in the uniform colors of corporate signage, so that all cities start to look alike and, wherever you go, the same uniformity dulls the eye.

When I see developers mow down hundred-year-old trees without a second thought to build boring and featureless buildings, I fear the worst.

In Montreal, for example, where green spaces are at a premium, I find it shameful that developers insist on encroaching on parks instead of doing something about all the modern ruins.

Architect friends have told me that more and more cities build streets in accordance with municipal bylaws designed to accommodate fire trucks. Isn't it strange that we're building cities according to the width of trucks instead of adapting trucks to the cities and the cities to their citizens?

I worry that our gaze will become inured to ugliness. That we'll forget that our cities are intended for humans to live in and enjoy. Let's create places that we inhabit, certainly, but also places that inhabit us. Places that inspire.

**Powerful Influences**

At last we've arrived in Brittany. I've been dying to get here.

I have two friends, Marielle and Isabelle, who come from this gorgeous land. They both have eyes the color of the sea, open features and pure hearts. They're model mothers and managers, and are for me a source of attachment to France. My ties with a country are always defined by my friendships.

The sea air of Saint Malo and Dinar, the long walks on the beach, the lovely children who seem to be healthier than anywhere else, all delighted me.

Motionless, my partner let his eyes scan the sea, the sand, the rocks, looking for traces of beauty.

He waited and watched, his finger cocked to snap the picture that would eternalize even the most fleeting beauty.

Good photography requires taking time to allow yourself to be surprised, to let beauty grab hold of you.
I'd like to let my gaze wander over the world with a photographer's eye searching out beauty.

I want beauty in the noblest sense of the word, marvelous creations in the magical sense of the word, and citizenship in the humanist sense of the word.

A large part of our imagination is marked by violence, famines, wars, competition and incomprehension.

We can see this clearly in the works of young contemporary artists. These works reflect our failures. Their messages are hard but clear.

It's up to us whether or not we want to hear them. The era of success, as it's been defined, doesn't suit everyone.

My day in that school talking with young people affected me deeply. Some gave me hope for tomorrow, others gave me cause to reflect on the legacy we're leaving them. I saw an instant image of our society. A snapshot of the best as well as the worst.

Older people who are disillusioned and without ideals may seem pathetic, but young people without ideals are a sad and ominous phenomenon.

It makes me want to stretch a large white canvas on the walls of every school, to help young people to dream, and to invite them to draw their dreams together.

At first I wanted to bring them all together, the gifted, the dropouts, the "unremarkable," so that they could blend their colors and dreams and create a single great canvas. I imagined a fresco.

But then I was afraid to attempt the experience, afraid that the dreams would be too dark — or too dreary — and would discourage them all the more.

Remember Sabato and Pessoa's lesson: dreams cannot lie.

I wish that we could relearn to dream with young people, that those of us who still have some enthusiasm would join them to imagine the society we want to create, instead of imposing our rules for success and performance on them, our addiction to consumption and our hunger for conquest.

By insisting so much on success, we end up provoking the opposite kind of behavior.

The law of the excluded is at work: the majority makes the least effort, while development is reserved for the most talented. We valorize the victims, and imprison them in secondary roles for their entire existence, instead of encouraging them to break free.

"For those of us who are gifted," young people who were doing well told me, "it's easy. It's the others you should encourage. We're okay, we're already highly motivated."

Despite the season's uncertain weather, Saint-Malo was bustling. Preferring deserted beaches to crowded ones, we managed from time to time to find a spot to ourselves. Why do people have this strange desire to congregate in the same places?

Early one Sunday morning, looking for silence and solitude, I went walking in Chateaubriand's estate. I stopped by the door of the small house where he was born, and recalled his words: "My life would become completely upset as soon as it was no longer mine."[4]

Since Venice, I had been going in the other direction. More than anything, I wanted to regain my freedom and fully assume the responsibility such freedom entails. At last I felt ready to follow Rilke's advice: "You must go inside yourself.... If there is an affirmative reply, if you can simply and starkly answer 'I must' to that grave question, then you will need to construct your life according to that necessity. Even in its most trivial and commonplace moments your life must be the expression of and the witness to that imperative."[5]

That weekend, caressed by wind and tired by my long walks, I found my spirit once again. After all, if we don't do it for ourselves, who will? To emulate someone, to want to be something, to surpass oneself, to create and to dedicate oneself to a cause that gives us more faith in humanity: these are the creative drives we should encourage in school, at work and in society as a whole.

At that moment, gazing out over the horizon, I was convinced that we could do it. Nothing was beyond hope. Especially since, "within the word hopelessness, we always find the word hope,"[6] as Anne-Lise Grobéty so cleverly points out.

My greatest desire is to participate with others in the creation of a world where there is still room for freedom, poetry and beauty.

In such a world, from our first days in school, we'd be taught to learn for ourselves, to educate our own gaze, like a muscle that we stretch more and more, to increase our ability to discover what is around us, to enrich it through the many visions we share and exchange.

We would come together in the search for intelligent solutions. We'd learn to learn from one another, and to be inspired by what happens in the most beautiful love stories, when two people endlessly surprise and give to each other. Our gaze is transformed in rediscovering the one we love. Isn't that the secret to a long life: to maintain that child's gaze in the search for new discoveries and beauty?

As children, we have that poetry within us. Little by little, we drift away from it. I would like the *School of Desires* to incite us to take the byways and hidden paths, to ramble the way we did as children. The *School of Desires* must encourage us to get back on that schoolchild's path and rethink our ways of learning and building.

In North America, the children of parents who are well-off are kept busy, from a young age. Their parents, in preparing them for life, want them to excel in sports, music, languages, mathematics and science. If nothing else, they'll excel at time management!

Idle moments are banished. And yet, my fondest memories of childhood are those times when I let my imagination wander, chasing butterflies. Those times during my vacations when I read for hours on end, when my mind roamed through universes that formed and grew as the hours passed. Those times when silence was my only companion.

Isn't free time a basic right of childhood? We need that time to develop an inner self, which will give us the drive to imagine and build in later years. It's a question of nurturing an imagination that will one day help us rebound from those inevitable difficult moments in our lives.

Doesn't the right to childhood really come down to these moments of happiness spent in calm surroundings conducive to tenderness?

We learn to be citizens long before the age of thirty. School should be a place of inspiration that communicates a thirst for knowledge and teaches us to discover and surpass ourselves. It should be a place that helps us to grasp the importance of small gestures. Each time I see an adult toss a cigarette butt on the sidewalk, or I spot a soda bottle floating on the river, I think civic responsibility should be one of the first things we're taught, so that it becomes an automatic reflex. We can all contribute to creating beauty, or at least to preserving that which already exists.

Without realizing it, we follow the trends of our era. During the industrial age, we created the factory-school, intended to produce graduates in large numbers. Our intentions were good: to make school available to all.

Unfortunately, along the way, as small problems arose, we sought complicated solutions. We conceptualized, intellectualized… forgetting that behind each problem, people wanted a simple answer that was easy to put into practice, rather than a bureaucratic program that would take years to demonstrate its ineffectiveness.

Efficiency demands modules or little boxes, or so we think. We specialize so much that little by little, our hearts and minds grow smaller. We stop thinking about anything but budgetary constraints and, little by little, our imaginations grow dull and the collective spirit dissipates.

We demand nothing less than A students. Performance is the name of the game. We want results immediately, if not sooner. Either students succeed according to the rules, or else they're utter failures. The risk is becoming a nobody. And we wonder why there are an ever-growing number of dropouts. I understand parents who opt for private schools, but meanwhile I think we're rapidly eroding the quality of public schools.

Teachers can't solve all of society's problems in their classrooms. In Quebec, where I'm more familiar with the situation, basic politeness seems to be reserved for an elite. So many young people don't even bother to be respectful of others.

Media glorification of stars also encourages this phenomenon. To succeed means to be #1, the big winner, rolling in money, a media darling. Anyone in the shadows is unworthy of our attention or admiration. As a result, some people are ready to do anything to grab the spotlight.

The experts sought sophisticated solutions to every problem, and the specialists tried to integrate all these solutions into programs, giving the teachers detailed instructions on how to proceed. Most do their best, hoping to improve the situation. But by intellectualizing the problems, we've only succeeded, despite our best intentions, in creating a complicated and unmanageable monster.

And all of us, whoever we are, exhaust ourselves at work trying to function within these incredibly complicated, sprawling systems. In the end, we're forced to face the facts. The results just aren't there. The number of professional burnouts is increasing, the rate of dropouts continues to rise. At least that's the situation in Quebec. More and more young people resort to suicide, and at a younger age. Senseless violence among young people is also on the rise. We're confronted by an unacceptable situation, powerless before a society which we built, but which is today beyond our control.

With the best intentions, we wanted to make education accessible to all, but we forgot that a school isn't just walls, a roof and some programs hatched by experts. Nor is a school a business, and it shouldn't be training people to merely follow orders, it should develop humanist creators. School should really be a place of desires: the desire to be, to learn, to create, to build, to share.

But to desire, we need free time, a slower pace, so that we can hear that quiet interior music that will set us in motion. Of course, I'm all for action and accomplishment, but I believe that moments of silence and tranquility are essential to achieve anything. What good is school if we don't play hooky once in a while? School must be rethought by not one but by many people, because it's the seed of a society which is created and renewed on the basis of shared dreams. That's why I hope we will work together to create the *School of Desires*, whose graduates become true citizens who contribute to building a society that is as original as our combined imaginations working together and our conjoined efforts can make it.

I'll be back, I told myself as I set out for the train station. From that first weekend in Brittany, I'd remember how I felt when I looked out at those beautiful landscapes, especially the cliffs of Dinar. And the beauty of the laughing children playing in the sand.

Saint-Malo, March 2002

FISSURE

"If we dream with grandeur, either we're crazy, we believe
in our dreams and are happy, or else we're just simple
dreamers for whom dreaming is the music of the soul,
rocking it gently without telling it anything.
But once we dream the possible, we also know
the real possibility of true disappointment."[1]

Fernando Pessoa

3

I was going home to Montreal for a few days, just long enough to see a few clients and to make headway on some strategic matters. In February, I'd told a client with whom I'd been working a long time that I wanted to end our collaboration. My heart just wasn't in it anymore. Not to mention my head.

I was ready to give them a few months to get organized, but my decision was final. It was a difficult time, because I had to continue serving them well, while knowing that I no longer believed in what they were doing.

All my life, I'd viewed my communications projects as ways to help groups evolve toward a more intelligent, more creative society.

On the one hand, I've never been able to consider financial success as true success. I've always assumed that profits and good financial results come if you work well, offering good services and products. It's just natural.

For me, however, the process is as important as the results. What we experience, what we feel, learn, create and share during a project seems to me to be as important as the financial profits that result.

On the other hand, pleasure is my drug. I have to have fun while I work and to feel that the same is true for those around me. I don't like working in a grim environment.

I aspire neither to fortune nor fame, but I do want happiness, freedom and the possibility to express myself. I want to participate, in some form or other, in the beauty of the world.

"Wherever on this earth I saw what we call happiness, I realized that it came from the richness of our impressions,"[2] wrote Hermann Hesse. Thus, at that moment, my greatest fear was that I might lose my ability to feel, hiding myself instead behind a wall that would render my senses lifeless, and my life senseless.

Over the years, the feeling of pleasure that I needed had dissipated. I could see that some of my clients took themselves and their business jargon too seriously, seeking nothing but profits, promotions and fame. I just couldn't see what they saw in all that.

I watched them become more and more focused on budgets, profits, meeting objectives and on their egos. I witnessed a growing demand for ever better results, with less and less attention to the artisans who made those results possible.

I felt what I can only describe as a lack of humanity. This seemed to me to be a step backward from past years. As a result, a kind of dichotomy began to grow between my heart and my head.

I had the skills and experience to contribute to improved results, but at the same time, I felt increasingly like an actor in a human comedy written by managers and politicians, each one defending his or her small lackluster dream (and often their personal power). On many mornings, I woke with a feeling of dread at the thought of the meetings that lay ahead of me that day.

It was a terrible realization, because, for the first time, I felt as though I was regretting my past. I had always acted out of passion and with all my heart; now I was putting all that into question, and I was unable to continue without feeling hypocritical.

Was it me who had changed to the point where my old projects no longer interested me? Or had society changed? Both had changed, of course, since life is movement, but I'm convinced that the external changes intensified the changes within me.

In fact, as I saw that society was going awry, I became more aware of my own desires and errors. I became more self-critical and tried to make choices that would help me refocus and improve myself.

I realized that, without my heart, my head could not go far. I had to transform this discovery into a creative rather than destructive act. That was the work before me.

More and more I agreed with the architect Mies van der Rohe's dictum that less is more, and I became profoundly convinced that we should apply it to everything, not just to architecture.

As I worked my way through this troubled time in my life, I began to feel a greater lightness and authenticity.

During those five days in Montreal, I was so absorbed by my thoughts that I remember neither the weather, nor the colors of the river and the sky.

I went from one meeting to the next, listening again and again to Daniel Bélanger's latest album, *Rêver Mieux* (Better Dreams): "And I believe everything comes, everything happens to those who know how to die, the better to be born again. Through the pain, I believe we come back better, having mourned our selves."[3] Over and over, Bélanger's words rose above the sounds of the engine and the traffic. To me, they were like a call to action.

A person of intellect creates complexity, a person of the heart refocuses and returns to what's essential. Isn't evolution a movement of trial and error until we achieve a kind of equilibrium, precarious yes, but an equilibrium nonetheless?

I wanted to work towards that equilibrium, so I could feel joy again. "I wake in the morning with a secret joy," Montesquieu wrote. "I see the light with a kind of rapture. All the rest of the day, I am happy."

That's how I wanted to live.

That year, as it does every year, spring followed on the heels of winter. If, after the cold and blizzards, there was new hope in the budding trees and sprouts, there might also be hope for me. I would have liked to forget those aspects of society that kept me from my desires. My one wild desire was to start over again.

Thinking about my past experiences, I recalled Marguerite Yourcenar's wonderful text on Rodin: "the work contains tempests of desire and the great calm of waiting; also, dreams that become acts, and acts that become dreams."[4] Being wrapped up in my own dreams and my actions, one of the beautiful surprises life has brought me was the idea of collective intelligences that I wrote about in *City of Intelligences*, and which I've continued to develop since.

Projects based on this approach have brought new desires and sometimes major transformations to a number of people. The testimonials I've received from those who took the time to write, often with poetic eloquence, have been like stars lighting a road sometimes darkened by doubts. Really it's for those people that I had to write this book of reflections. I wanted to share not just some of my disillusionments, but also the hopes I continue to harbor. I wanted to invite them to continue their struggle even if it means running counter to the current trend.

I wanted to tell them that I too have noticed the change in the wind's direction, but that it's only made me work all that much harder. I've simply decided to tackle the problem differently.

Let's lay the foundations for the *School of Desires*. We owe that much to our children. Before telling our children what to do, shouldn't we begin by trying to do it ourselves? I sometimes feel that we've run out of ideas; we have the capitalist model as a kind of template, and we try to apply it to everything: the family, education, school, leisure activities. And yet, our best teachers may be our children.

The leaders of businesses and other organizations are our creations. They are the products of what they've learned in school and society, and of our expectations. Our gaze is their mirror; it contributes to making them what they are.

Parents apply what they learn in their place of work at home. The children of the well-off in this era of performance are proof of that. Some people even use their children as a means to enhance their social status.

Once again, we follow the collective movement. Our neighbor does it, our colleague does it; we do it too, without necessarily taking the time to think. Our surroundings influence us.

During my seminars on leadership, which are really creativity workshops, I see leaders becoming aware of how they got into their present situation — and seeing their mistakes. Some of them want to contribute in a different way.

They often emerge from these seminars with renewed energy, but they tell me they find it difficult to inspire others to do the same. We're the products of the society we live in. We're carried along by the current, in the wake of the crowd moving toward a single objective. It's not easy to resist.

What's more, so few of us have been educated in the spirit of collective intelligences. "In the West," Pierre Faure writes, "whether the model is the transcendent God of the Bible or the Platonic world of ideas… This spirit of domination, pushed to the limit, has produced the results we all know, including hypertrophy of the self and the destructive conquest of nature."[5]

Which is why it's so important to take time off, to get some perspective on the way we're managing our lives and businesses. Workshops always have their difficult moments, but mainly they provide moments of happiness and surprise. The magic comes from the sincere willingness of the participants to play the game, to really reconsider their methods and, more importantly, to let go and reveal oneself while discovering others.

It's a game that produces collective creations and demonstrates the extraordinary creativity of people who have confidence in themselves. It's not possible to properly convey these experiences in a book, because the work belongs to each participant. Each workshop is a collective.

Because so many participants expressed a desire to pass on this sort of experience to others, I decided to share my idea of how to foster collective creation and the magical moments it affords.

The idea of collective leadership is similar in some ways to the organization of traditional societies which, according to Pierre Clastre, still exists among the indigenous people of Uruguay: "the position of chief is held in turn by different members of the tribe, and its function consists not in exercising power, but in making sure no one takes power. It's as though the position of sovereign was left empty here, a place left vacant by choice, of which the individual is merely the guardian."[6]

What I like about this idea is the possibility of educating our gaze to see otherwise, and then to contribute to reshaping reality according to our discoveries.

It's a new way of looking that entails less quick judgments and less incomprehension between communities, between worlds that still seem irreconcilable to us today.

We need to take time out to find ways to rekindle desire in each of us. We need prescriptions to educate our eyes so that they become seekers of beauty.

We need to take time out to educate our ears to hear in new ways, so that our spirit hungers for new discoveries, especially if these discoveries lead us a thousand miles from our certainties.

The quest for desires applies to all of us. As Noëlle Barbot writes, "desire needs to be desired."[7]

And I would add… power needs to be shared.

Ernesto Sabato writes: "Through bloody struggles, colonialisms and empires of every stripe have pulverized traditions and profaned values that had stood for thousands of years, reducing nature and human desires to the level of trifling objects."[8]

It's time we resist. Let's replace the spirit of conquest with the quest for desires. That is absolutely the spirit of my collective intelligence approach. In the next chapter I'll try to present it to you in the simplest terms, so that it might become yours, if you so desire.

As you can see, in spite of some disappointments, I've chosen to dream grand dreams and to believe in my dreams so long as I know they're shared by others.

Montreal, April 2002

A PLURAL INTELLIGENCE

"He allowed characters and groups to locate themselves;
he observed the life of the people he had created,
he watched and treated each individual according to their will."[1]

Marguerite Yourcenar, on Auguste Rodin

4

I was in Paris again, with a few days to prepare a seminar. Ah, the silence and solitude — I really appreciated these precious moments that let me go deep into myself.

I tried to set aside some quiet time for myself before the seminar, an event that was bound to surprise me as much as the participants, since it was designed as a process of collective reflection through creativity games.

This luxury of one or two days before a workshop was something new. Of late, I'd had the desire to let time do its work.

Impatience being one of my faults, I've lived much of my life trying to cram as many activities as possible into every hour. It was a need, a necessity, a kind of surfeit, or something I did to please others or something I did simply out of curiosity: the reason didn't matter.

At that hour of the afternoon, my office was bathed in bright sunlight. I was rereading Rilke's *Letters to a Young Poet* once again. As I sat at my desk, each word resonated with special meaning.

One passage stuck in my mind as particularly apt. "To allow each thing its own evolution, each impression and each grain of feeling buried in the self, in the darkness, unsayable, unknowable, and with infinite humility and patience to await the birth of a new illumination: this alone is what it means to live the life of an artist — in understanding as much as in creating."[2]

Like caterpillars, those friends of my childhood, I felt myself mutating into something new. It was as though I was shedding my skin.

I was no longer interested in affirming, convincing, leading. I wanted to make myself available, to be alert to my inner self, to the silence of others, to their hearts, rather than letting myself be carried away by the same old discourses. In any case, it had been awhile since I had been able to listen to them without picking them apart and reading between the lines to decipher the calculations and politics under the surface.

My new state was certainly linked to the particular circumstances of my life. But it had also come out of my discussions with my good friend in France, Sylvie, who had contributed to my reflections on the ego, and given me a new appreciation of the works of Hermann Hesse and Rilke. The result was a growing desire for wisdom and happiness.

It was in this transitory state, almost of mutation, that I prepared myself for what turned out to be a wonderful experience.

They were ten, all managers. We were to spend three days together at the Chalet des Îles in Bois de Boulogne, on the outskirts of Paris. Every morning, we crossed the small lake to gather together and discuss the qualities of a manager, and how we could work differently inside the company, reinventing ways to communicate and to successfully manage innovative projects.

In spite of some skepticism, even cynicism, at first, we rapidly established a climate of confidence and goodwill. Those who are well aware of the gap between institutional discourses and reality can be hesitant to invest themselves in such a process. It's true that senior management can sometimes frustrate the feelings of their collaborators.

But I believe we have to seize every opportunity to participate in creative and thought-provoking experiences. If the company doesn't take advantage of them, too bad for the company. The participants will benefit, in any case, in other areas of their lives.

Having said this, I can easily understand people's initial hesitations. But I'm convinced — and I have the testimony to prove it — that those who deny themselves the chance to fully participate in such an experience end up punishing themselves more than their company management.

The results of this particular seminar were fabulous. I was moved by the participants' sensitivity, intelligence and creativity. It was yet another demonstration that, when participants sincerely involve themselves in the conversation and creative games, the workshops can become magical moments of collective genius.

Alone in my office, preparing the content of such seminars, I have an idea of how it will go, of course, but what I find most stimulating is to allow myself to be surprised and swept up in moments of beauty. It's absolutely moving to see my intuitions confirmed, to see the proof that a few people can, in a very short time, share their desires and dreams, think about which values are important to defend, and create the possibility of doing things differently, better, more humanely.

What really struck me was that though we were in enchanting surroundings, the real enchantment took place within four walls. Our work inside was so intense that the smokers even forgot to slip outside for a cigarette. That speaks volumes.

Aside from the crossing of the lake every morning and evening, our surroundings didn't contribute very much to the magic. If we open our hearts, we find inspiration within us and bring it to others. It's the most crucial element, and the most difficult.

If more management teams participated in such adventures, managers would be better leaders and learn to manage differently. The more that people began to do so, the better it would be for society.

It requires an open mind and courage just to participate in these workshops. You can't be afraid to remove the mask you may have taken years to perfect.

The workshop helps managers to practice a kind of leadership that encourages, enlightens, listens, informs, retraces and recognizes: a leadership that fosters complicity.

But beware: a manager is not a psychiatrist. He or she wasn't trained to be one. As an employee, I wouldn't expect that of my boss. Respect requires that we maintain a certain distance.

The truth is I've never met anyone who has succeeded in changing another person. The work on oneself is the work of a lifetime. Others can inspire us, encourage us, make us think; they're a kind of mirror in front of us, but the work on oneself remains infinitely personal and private.

A leader can only work on the context. He or she can create an atmosphere conducive to the respect of certain basic values.

The idea of the seminar is not to give people the prescriptions of experts; it simply allows participants to experience moments of collective creation. These moments demonstrate the importance of context and the results that can be quickly obtained, while providing a lot of pleasure for all those involved.

During workshops, there are always those who feel a symbiotic relationship to the ideas, and contribute to accelerating the group's evolution toward a process of collective intelligence.

Others resist, but gradually realize the value of frank exchanges. With the help of the first group, they become more authentic.

It can be extremely stimulating to set political games aside for a while, along with the prejudices we have about each other.

Some managers may not want to do this kind of work, preferring to sit in their ivory towers with their old habits and certainties, never putting any of them into question.

## School of Desires

It's essential to respect each person's desires and degree of progress. As the old Chinese saying goes, the master appears when the pupil is ready.

For my part, I'm learning not to push, not to force things. I try to guide rather than direct. I'm learning to listen to the group and its dynamics so that the group decides as freely as possible how the work will be done.

The only role of authority I exercise is that of timekeeper and guardian of the values we have agreed to respect as long as we're together.

That evening, after the workshop, I was strolling alone in Paris to let the powerful emotions of the day settle. And I was thinking that the beautiful moments we experience during a workshop could, and should, be part of the daily life of companies.

Wouldn't society as a whole benefit if a greater number of people were fulfilled in their work and allowed to be more creative, if they were listened to and had more opportunities to demonstrate their intelligence?

Managing a team is an enormous responsibility, which we should look upon as a calling, in the way we are called by a vocation or an artistic passion.

Obviously, when we speak of leadership, we are talking about human qualities. The best leaders are exceptional people who demonstrate authenticity, humility, courage, integrity, curiosity and empathy. First and foremost they are respectful. Respectful of themselves, of others and of nature. And they're usually generous.

The most dedicated among them work at developing their emotional intelligence and abilities such as vision, a good communications sensibility, active listening, and rigor. They know how to follow up so that everyone understands the big picture. They're good guides, good at scouting new terrain. They don't change their priorities every day. They stay the course when it comes to the essentials. They keep the framework uncluttered.

Contrary to what many people think, managers who obtain the best and lasting results, are not the most flamboyant, nor the most charismatic. They're not selling anything or trying to convince, they're apprentices, much like the best teachers, who continue to learn from their students. They encourage those around them to achieve results together by surpassing themselves as a group. They show the way.

Studies on leadership have shown that the departure of the best managers often goes unnoticed because the team continues to function without them. They've been able to share their values, knowledge, savoir-faire, and shape a collective spirit, so that even the loss of the leader does not affect overall results.

Managers who issue orders to others without respecting them may obtain compliance but never the commitment of intelligent people who feel recognized for their contributions. It's collective ideas and the participation of every person that lets a company achieve the highest profits.

A CEO who's a good talker can make the cover of the magazines for a while but, once that manager has moved on, analysis will often uncover disasters.

Shouldn't CEOs take a few minutes of their precious time to ask themselves what sort of leader they want to be?

From Socrates to Shakespeare, from "Know thyself" to "Who am I?" the questions we ask ourselves in the course of a lifetime have nothing to do with fashions and trends.

They're the very essence of every human life. Neither technology nor our so-called modernity will change them.

**Emotional Intelligence**

**Humility**

**Curiosity**

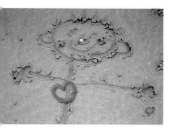
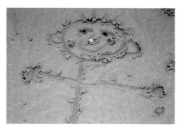
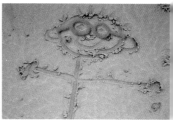

### A Plural Intelligence

In fact, true leadership is encouraging others to do extraordinary things. And we require neither a title nor a particular function to exercise it. Others give us that power.

In their book, *The Future of Leadership*, James M. Kouzes and Barry Z. Posner cite the example of Melissa Poe, a nine year old girl from Nashville who, worried by the destruction of our planet's resources, launched a campaign in her school to "Protect the Environment for Future Generations."

Because she felt she herself had little power, Melanie wrote to the President of the United States, asking him to endorse her cause. To attract his attention, she managed to have her letter published on 250,000 neon signs in various American cities.

**Integrity**

**Empathy**

**Grandiloquence**

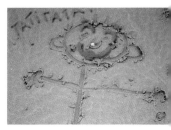

Instead of the President's support she'd hoped for, hundreds of children offered their help. Nine months later, she created *Kids for a Clean Environment*, which now has more than 200,000 members. The group designs programs and manuals for schools to foster the protection of the environment. Now that's an example of leadership. It's really quite simple.

This is the kind of act we discuss during our seminars. We reflect on the "positive" power that each of us could exercise. It's our duty, if we hope to build a society that stands together, to encourage each other to step forward and be counted on worthwhile issues.

Every company must, along with conducting its business, contribute to developing social and ethical consciousness, and have its own employees participate actively. A collective conscience develops through direct experience, and it's not about making a huge media splash.

My seminars also offer participants an artistic experience, whether in painting, writing or theatre, so as to draw them away from their hyper-rational way of thinking and bring them closer to the creative act.

It's also a chance to leave part of your ego at the door, since everyone is identified only by their first name.

The best groups are composed of people of varying ages and types. Differences make for greater openness.

My workshops are an invitation to think and talk about life, society and the values we hold dear.

It's a moment of collective commitment to make work a stimulating, creative and ethical experience. It's a process of collective creation whose results are similar to those obtained in art-therapy programs.

To visualize how a collective intelligence process works, picture an apple tree:

1. The roots represent our creative desire. What do roots need in order to grow? Space, air, water, time and sunlight. In order to desire, we too need spaces of freedom, leisure time, oxygen and silence. Our first responsibility to ourselves is to provide our desires with this vital minimum.

We have to protect our private space of desires. It's more than a question of survival; it's a question of living one's life as fully as possible. The ideal, of course, is to succeed in coupling one's personal desires with professional accomplishments.

2. The trunk represents the foundation, that is, our dreams. If we let our desires emerge, they become waking dreams we can share with others. They are the force and power that drive us to act.

Just as the trunk grows upward to bear and sustain branches, so do dreams try to take shape so they can exist in the world as dreams-come-true. We are just as much waking dreamers as we are dreamers when we sleep; the images in our imagination are like seeds we sow in order to build reality and provide us coherent meaning.

3. The branches are the common language we must develop between us to communicate. They are the words, sounds, images that we retain to speak of our desires and our dreams.

In another sense, they are the metaphors, signs, and symbols that help to provide unity to this individual and plural cacophony.

Finally, they are the myths, rituals and legends that unite us. In this way, we all become creators of content and stories; we all become storytellers.

The leaves represent the results of our experimentation. They are a visual reminder of the attempts that allow us to progress. Some leaves grow and turn green, others fall; it's all part of the game. Some dreams come true, while others fail. Too much planning can be a waste of time; it's in action that we find out if the tree will bear fruit. The fruit is the harvest — and it's our effort, our determination and our perseverance in trying to incarnate our dreams that gives us the most beautiful apples.

The climate in which our tree grows can make all the difference. There must be benevolence, respect, and — I dare to add — love.

If we maintain a dialogue through all the stages, we will bring more creative and more ethical products and services to market that truly have added value. In so doing, we'll be "contributors to society," since we'll have come to an understanding at the outset on the essential values to defend in the world we invent and build together. In this way, we'll be conscious of our collective power.

**All Dreamers**

**All Creator-storytellers**

**All Actors**

When *City of Intelligences* came out in France, I gave a talk at the Conservatory of Arts and Crafts, where I met Mathieu Baudin, a young French idealist with a head full of dreams and a contagious desire to live. It was the beginning of 2000.

Mathieu had been struck by my approach and wanted to write his doctoral thesis on the collective intelligence process. He has since been one of its ardent defenders. He came to Quebec to see my projects. He met participants two years later. He had just been hired as an intern, in France, to map out a project which we then launched.

The difficulty is that, apart from some relatively short-lived experiences, we had no concrete example lasting over a sufficiently long period, at least to my thinking. There have been attempts, but nothing that fully measured up to the respect for human values on which the approach relies.

Meanwhile, in 2002, I'd begun to question my own approach. I realized that it could be used to seduce or manipulate, contrary to what I'd intended.

My utopian dream was to see companies become cities of intelligences. I believed with all my heart, and had spent a great deal of energy trying to prove that this vision could help us evolve toward a more humane society.

It's not that I no longer believe, but I have become aware of the truth of Lord Acton's maxim: "Power tends to corrupt, and absolute power corrupts absolutely."

This said, I know from the many touching responses to my seminars that they did contribute to awakenings that bore fruit in many aspects of peoples' lives. Still, I was not able to measure the results in the ways I would have wished.

We live in a bean-counting society that wants a rapid return on investment. Marketing is expected to produce instant success. As a North American, I too like speedy results; I like efficiency and pragmatism. What I don't like are dream merchants. Life has taught me that any true apprenticeship requires enormous patience. Profound change doesn't come with lightning speed. Mentalities don't alter with a snap of the fingers. We need courage and perseverance.

In our fast-paced world, it's not easy to sell the idea that results require time and patience, but it's honest. And, if at first we don't succeed, as the saying goes, we must try, try again. We have to work on it daily. My experiences have taught me a great lesson in humility. I used to say repeatedly that "anything is possible." Today, I think it's essential to desire and to do one's best. That done, we can view how the situation unfolds, and see what we can learn from it, in order to improve our next collective creations.

I learned that everything comes in its own time.
For someone who's chronically impatient,
it was no small lesson!

It's true that I was often naïve, but how could I have been otherwise? Some people get through life by scoffing at the world. I have only my ideals to rely on. Even today, I have my doubts about certain companies. Which is why I'm addressing my readers as individuals to help make the *School of Desires* a reality. Couldn't such a project be a collective effort, created in the street, in groups, in families, between friends, and not only in the halls of power?

I was talking about it that weekend with an extraordinary man to whom Mathieu had introduced me, Andrès Andrade, a humanist as visionary as Pablo Neruda. Today Andrès divides his time between Chile and France.

In his youth, Andrès was an airline pilot. One day, preparing to take off for Cuba, he learned that the revolution had triumphed there. Quickly he offered to let his American passengers off to take another flight, to New York, and took on board all the Cubans who wanted to go home to their country.

When the plane landed, Che's soldiers came on board to greet them. Andrès was so moved by their welcome that he decided to offer his services to the General. He left his homeland Chile, and his well paid job. His family followed him in this great adventure.

In Cuba, he helped to train pilots and founded a flying school. His discussions with Che Guevara are among his treasured memories.

He told me how he'd involved people in decision-making. For a while the results were excellent, until the new leadership decided to import Russian Communism with its dogmas and rules, which did nothing to encourage people to think for themselves. Andrès became disillusioned. He was expelled from Cuba and went to live in England, where he completed a Masters degree at the University of London.

My question may seem stupid: Why must things that begin with such hope so often go so wrong?

What makes them veer off course? It's as though, as soon as we give people a bit of dignity, as soon as they are allowed to participate in decisions and made responsible for the society in which they live, some power-hungry madman has to ruin it all.

That day over coffee with Andrès, my confidence returned. We were hoping to work together. One day, maybe we will… Andrès is a young man of 80. I hoped that life would bring a project my way that would let both of us work together to arouse the desire to adopt approaches of collective intelligence. He's been on the ground in different countries than I have. His examples are food for thought, especially if we want to draw lessons from the past before imagining the future.

The following Sunday, I woke early, satisfied with my week in Paris. I took advantage of my last hours of rest to stroll on the Île Saint-Louis and in the gardens of the Louvre. At the end of the afternoon, I had tea in one of those tearooms unique to

Paris, with their hushed atmosphere that draws you into the past.

Then I went to see Ron Howard's wonderful film, *A Beautiful Mind*. When I emerged, the Champs-Elysées was full of crowds. I made my way slowly back home, thinking that so much effort could not be in vain. There were probably a lot more exceptional people than I thought. I only had to do a better job at finding them.

I still believe in the collective intelligence approach, but to bring it to fruition we need a great many exceptional people, people who agree to share power and rely on the intelligence of each individual.

We need men and women ready to defend the values of tolerance, respect, dignity, freedom, honesty and fraternity, the only values that will let us build our schools, businesses, cities, and society together.

Paris, April 2002

EYES WIDE OPEN

"Let us give ourselves eyes that see clearly…"[1]

Ingres

5

When I got back to Montreal at the end of April, the city was in the grip of a heat wave. It was as hot as if it were July. My country is a land of extremes. It shapes our character.

At the first sign of spring, when the snow's barely melted, people are quick to shed their winter clothing. The game of seduction begins on every street corner and in the first outdoor cafés to open.

The air is so frenetic you'd think we'd all swallowed some kind of euphoric drug. At last winter's really over. We're like new shoots busting out of the ground. Nature takes over.

To me, it's as though we were making symbolic gestures to attract the sun and heat.

As though shedding layers of clothes so quickly would somehow magically stop the cold from returning.

A French friend, with whom I was walking on St-Denis Street that day, observed that women in Montreal were rather scantily dressed. I wasn't sure what to say. All I know is that we go directly from the polar to the tropical, at dramatic speed. It's as visible in the faces as in the clothes.

I was happy rediscovering my city and my river. I rose with the sun, and took up my old habit of morning walks. I savored the comfort of my apartment, suspended in that magnificent sky that I miss whenever I'm away from it for too long.

I felt like writing. It was my way to reestablish a kind of internal calm. I'd been getting lovely messages from people in France and Italy who wanted to work with me, because they too believed the dream of collective intelligence was possible. Every day, I printed the most beautiful messages and put them in my journal, knowing that, on dark days, they would light my way.

I'm grateful for the invention of the Internet. Who would have thought that one day I could communicate so easily with people all over the world. Even though my replies are brief, I'm always touched by the mail I get. I'm impressed that people take the time to confide how a book or a seminar changed something in their lives. I'm grateful to them. This book of reflections is, in part, dedicated to them.

I had a dream that I could one day bring them all together in the same country to share and create something new collectively. I think it would be fascinating. Of course, such a meeting could also take place in each of our imaginations, and become a reality in the work of many *Schools of Desires* established all over the world. Clearly, age hasn't slowed down my dreaming!

One thing's for sure, I felt like continuing the struggle, but more quietly. I had decided to smile. Simply this: to smile.

I told myself that, confronted with glazed, cynical or stressed faces, or even those ironic, calculating, political gazes, if I remained true to my desires I would always be able to smile.

I don't mean the sort of smile that communicates something, or that smile of American optimism described by Hermann Hesse, but rather an internal smile, not necessarily visible to others. This smile would let me keep things in perspective, would produce an internal peace, a hidden happiness. This would be my new weapon.

Although normally smiling comes naturally to me, when I read too many newspapers and start analyzing the world too closely, dark thoughts will put a frown on my face. I worry about young people. I get depressed about who we are, who we are becoming. I think too much; the future seems bleak, and I become disenchanted. At such times I try to remind myself that, in any case, life is fleeting. We're only passing through.

I think too of the ancient founding myths in which dragons become princesses at the last minute, if the hero has the courage to face the ultimate test. After all, doesn't change come in quantum leaps? That helps me to put the present, reality, suffering and injustice in perspective.

People told me: "You've changed." I nodded, smiling. I was pleased to see others no longer saw me as the fighter I once was. It pleased me, even though I knew it wasn't necessarily a compliment.

We live in a society where fighters are appreciated; we admire people who succeed thanks to the strength of their fists. In the future I would aspire to an internal form of combat, a life of lightness. I longed to be in harmony with the world, visible and invisible.

In other words, I no longer felt like breaking down doors; I preferred to step lightly through those that opened for me, leaving the others closed, without regret. I wanted to feel as though I were riding on the wings of a large soaring bird.

I can understand how, to others, such a transformation can seem strange. I myself was destabilized by it and even, at times, afraid.

These were the thoughts that accompanied me on my spring walks in Montreal. I went out very early in the day to enjoy the quiet in the city. I went to the Botanical Gardens where nature was gently waking.

I felt things had begun to change for me since Venice but, really, it had started on the day my mother died, Saturday, October 17, 1998. That morning, a pale sun illuminated her white bed. Through the window of her hospital room, I remember seeing a tree rocking gently in the wind, but I no longer know if I invented it or if it was there.

At exactly 8:10 that morning, she said goodbye to me, with such grace, with a face so full of light and love that, all the rest of that day, it was as though I was being carried along on a cloud. I wasn't cold, nor did I feel like crying; I was warmed by a gentle breath that enveloped my entire being from within.

Watching her during the last moments of her life, I wanted only one thing — and this may seem foolish — I felt a single powerful desire to be better. To do my best from now on. As though, without speaking, she'd communicated to me the enormous value of the goodness she had radiated throughout her lifetime. What's essential in what we leave behind us is just this, the elegance of the heart: love.

It was like a final generous gesture on the part of someone who had always loved and encouraged me. I was tremendously moved that she'd found the strength to come out of a three-day coma to pass on this final love potion.

I'd always been attracted to good rather than evil, not out of fear or duty, but simply by preference. But that day, I received a confirmation of my choice. A visceral reinforcement, like a gift she left me gently at the foot of her bed before departing. It was magical and marvelous, without a trace of sadness.

I'm still astonished at how calm I remained that entire day, in the company of my sisters. Our lips were graced with gentle smiles and, between us, there was a complicity woven out of our happiest memories and the ties of love she had always hoped to see between her children.

Of course, it couldn't last. By nightfall, pain and grief caught up with me. My tears, in spite of my sweetheart's consoling presence, followed for several months afterward.

But I'll never forget that first joyous day of mourning, nor this new inner strength which, thanks to her, was now mine.

That day marked the start of my self-questioning.

I felt her absence so strongly, and the loss of her gentle presence was so painful, that I left my country, thinking I could leave my grief behind. Eight months after her death, my Parisian adventure had begun and my gradual transformation was slowly taking place, day and night. When I couldn't sleep, I projected my worries on the white walls of my minimalist room: a small bed, a night table and a reading lamp were all I needed to imagine the future.

Three years later, lounging in my wide Montreal bed, I think back to that time of voluntary simplicity; which allowed me to return to what is essential. I'm glad that I learned then that we shouldn't let ourselves be weighed down by things or events. Life is both infinitely more complicated and simpler than that.

That was as far as I'd gotten in my thinking when Marielle — a wonderful woman who worked with me during my Paris seminars — emailed me photos of the three days we'd spent at Chalet des Îles. I could see the light in the eyes and smiles of the participants. It was tangible proof that I hadn't imagined it. The magic had really taken place again.

Foremost in my mind was to ensure the momentum would not be lost, so that once back in their workplaces, the participants would remain open to others and their ideas. How to help them maintain clear objectives and, more importantly, act quickly before the flame died down again? In my seminars, I'd often witnessed these magical moments, only to be disappointed a few years later by the lack of sustainable results. Even today, I'm convinced that this approach is far from having reached its full potential.

To agree on common values, to share a dream, to participate collectively in writing a scenario, to experiment — all in a climate of respect, goodwill and pleasure: that much we were able to do in three days. But I knew that the participants shared my concerns: how to get others on board, how to produce results year after year?

### School of Desires

At the top of the list of conditions for the success of any project is vision. One must have the courage to see the present for what it is, and realistically anticipate the future, but also the capacity to dream that future, to imagine it.

According to inventor Dr. Louis Taillefer, the most important quality in a researcher is imagination.

The same is true for most of us, even if we are only imagining our own lives.

As far back as I can remember, I've always dreamed; I'm sure I've spent as much time imagining my life as living it.

Many of my visions have become reality in one form or other, particularly those that I took the time to imagine in detail, to script and to project like a film in my mind.

All this has a lot to do with the inner eye and desire. It is as if two transparent films were juxtaposed: the series of fleeting impulses at the source of every dream, and the initial stirrings at the root of desire. Viewed together, they produce a flow of coherent images.

I often think that I only need to desire something in order for the world around me to show me the path to fulfilling it. Not always immediately, of course, nor always in the form I anticipated, but the core of the initial desire is always there.

This may seem like magical thinking, but it really isn't. My questioning is intended to better understand the way we learn, how our brain functions and how the potential creator in us develops.

Of course, some desires will never be realized. But it's often because, over time, we ourselves abandon them. We lose interest, or simply lose the need for desire. In this way, life can surreptitiously lose its intensity, run dry or fade away for years before it finally departs for good. Unless we replace old desires with new ones.

To live fully is to desire madly. It is to accept disorder, to decide continually what we want and what we no longer want.

Some days our desires become mixed up, like our ideas; misfortune is entangled with happiness, suffering with joy…

And time passes. We get lost in the daily grind. We even forget to desire. Sometimes we have to immerse ourselves in silence, solitude or suffering, in order to find new dreams within, to discover the hidden face of nascent desires.

We go into ourselves to see from within. How can I describe this kind of seeing? I have searched for a word that would distinguish it from mere seeing, just as you might combine "to Listen" and "to Hear." And I wanted a word with the notion of desire in it as well.

The word I wanted, in fact, already existed. It's a word that expresses the importance of the depth of a look; it marks a state or condition rather than a verb.

In fact, it's an activity I enjoy very much. You can do it for long periods of time, looking at nature or art. Or at people, but you'd better be discreet, or you'll risk getting on their nerves (or giving them the wrong idea).

The word is the noun from the same stem as the familiar verb "to gaze." It is *gazer*.

My mother often used to tell me: "Stop staring at people like that." Despite her scolding, I found it difficult to turn away. I would be fascinated with a small detail, a beautiful deep wrinkle, a particular expression. Mesmerized, I would forget that this detail belonged to a person who probably didn't appreciate my inquisitor's gaze.

In *The Legend of the Centuries,* Victor Hugo writes, "I am the infinite gazer." If only it were a profession! As a matter of fact, it's a state that's crucial for many professions, among them writer, painter and sculptor. It's also the first quality of a leader.

To be a gazer means to relearn to see each day.

I sometimes shut my eyes and then see differently when I reopen them. My memory and my gaze speak to each other. They work together to clarify the things and events of my life. As soon as I take the time to pause, as soon as I blink my eyes to see anew, I see something different.

**To see something different is to understand something different.** I was amused to read in a photography magazine that a banal snapshot of a winter snowstorm had been taken for a photograph of the collapse of New York City's World Trade Center on September 11. Unable to imagine snow whirling in the sky, the viewer had seen dust and ash. For us in Quebec, the image is just an ordinary photo of a snowbound city. A peaceful scene. We would never mistake it for ashes, and a picture of disaster.

Each of us sees things, landscapes, and people differently. Sharing interpretations and memories is what makes collective creations ripe with possibilities.

Every day we have opportunities to see differently. A child or poet can easily open our eyes. So can Nature. "Adults invent the past, because they have ideas in place of eyes," Boris Cyrulnik writes in *A Marvelous Misfortune*.[2]

We have to borrow the eyes of children to keep the dream alive from day to day. We also have to think about sharing it. We need to make it possible for others to see the dream by finding metaphors to help draw it better, photograph it better, and rekindle those childhood emotions and color our memories. We must keep our eyes alive.

When in Montreal, I often think of the importance of the gaze, because this city where I was born seems different each time I return. My gaze is renewed. Thanks to this going and coming back, I rediscover the freshness of first sightings, as I look at things I first observed long ago.

What we believe to be the truth is merely an interpretation, one way of seeing.

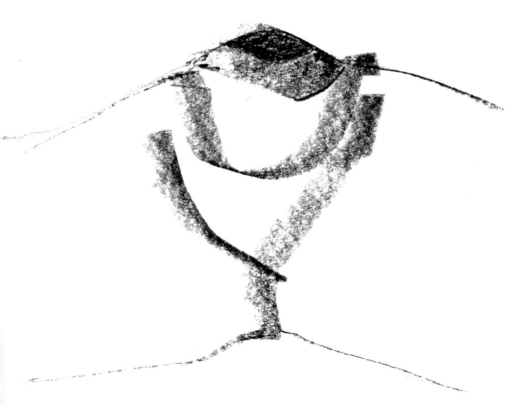

Love, memory, desire, nature, art, beauty, and encounters with others all help us to create eyes that see well.

French singer Juliette Gréco puts it nicely: "I am like the eyes of flies; I too have a thousand facets."[3] To look from within with the eyes of the heart, then from outside as a simple observer, to see close up or from afar — it doesn't matter, so long as we take the time to be a gazer. And so long as we dare to change our gaze by borrowing other people's glasses.

Hermann Hesse recounts a Chinese legend about an old master who exercised by standing on his head. He told his disciples: "The world seems fresher and more beautiful when I stand on my head." Since the people were always attentive to his teachings, the news and the practice quickly spread throughout the community. When the master returned, he told them: "What luck that humans have two legs! Standing on your head is bad for your health. Furthermore, the world looks twice as beautiful to he who rights himself and stands again on his own two feet." His disciples were furious that their master had proffered contradictory advice. He replied: "My dear children, there is a reality that nothing can shake, and then there are an infinite number of truths, which are only visions of reality; they are all equally true and false."[4]

When we change our gaze, we allow our eyes to wander in multiple universes and our imagination to travel. It's the diversity of our gazes that makes collective creations so inspiring.

It's also an excellent way to learn tolerance. If it's true that we construct reality on the basis of our perceptions — as many physicists believe — it's that much more important, as the painter Ingres said, to create eyes that see with wisdom.

Montreal, April 2003

LOSS OF ILLUSIONS

"Beauty is fragile… It arises on the crest of an instant. The slightest negligence, and it vanishes. And so many brutal, cruel elements come to crush it."[1]

François Cheng

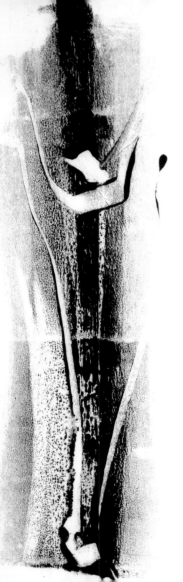

6

On returning from Vietnam, photographer Michel Laurent wrote to his wife, "What I've lost in illusions, I've gained in tenderness."[2] To me, this phrase is very beautiful and wise. It was a phrase I hoped to remember in my moments of disappointment.

At times, the loss of illusions can leave traces of bitterness that do neither us nor the world any good. I like the idea of replacing that bitter taste with tenderness.

Despite having a lot of work to do, I was enchanted by the spring. But once I was back inside the editing studio, looking at the footage we had shot in the school, I felt a twinge inside.

Listening to the comments of the young people, I heard them as a criticism of our past actions. I took their remarks seriously. I decided to sound the alarm in my scheduled presentation to the Quebec School Board commissioners.

The organizing committee responsible for setting up the conference was composed of people who were really passionate about improving Quebec's schools. They had the spirit of true reformers. Their enthusiasm had convinced me to accept their invitation.

I was also thrilled that researchers at the *School of the Future* of the University of Sâo Paulo in Brazil, an interdisciplinary laboratory investigating new communications technologies and their impact on learning at all educational levels, had read *City of Intelligences* and, in the summer of 2001, had decided to base their work on my collective intelligence approach.

By chance I'd met the coordinator of the project, Maria F. Mello, in Paris, at the home of my friend Michel Random, a writer, photographer and filmmaker.

Who could have predicted that after this chance meeting, my approach would inspire a university in Brazil in their project to reinvent schools!

In Brazilian culture, the use of metaphors is more part of the culture than it is in the North. South Americans are major creators of fantasy literature. They're used to switching rapidly between abstractions and concrete images, between the visible and the invisible. They are comfortable rubbing shoulders with the world of the marvelous and the imagination.

Their project was fascinating, and I dreamed of a similar experience in Quebec. When, several months later, I received a letter from Jean-Guy Boudrault — Chair of the upcoming annual general meeting of Quebec School Boards, and himself head commissioner of a school board, and a researcher in education — it was like a sign.

If companies are potential ground for experimentation, schools would seem to me to lend themselves even more to innovation. They ought to inspire business, rather than the reverse. But that would require courage; and some flexibility in existing structures.

It was with much hope — and great expectations on all sides — that our adventure began in the fall of 2001.

To ensure the meeting with the commissioners would be more than a catalogue of ideas — a mere intellectual exercise among managers — I suggested we allow young people to participate in our dream of a school of the future. That was the reason for my day visit to a high school in early winter of 2002, and for the camera that we'd brought along to preserve a record of the event.

What I hadn't predicted was the complete lack of desires among young people. Maybe I should have known, but I didn't. After that day in school, I was stumped. Some of those faces were so dull, so passive. There was so little demand for happiness. What had become of their dreams?

Playing and replaying the videotapes, I became so dejected that even the tenderness of early spring couldn't raise my spirits.

I can still see the large dark eyes of one young girl as she asked, "Couldn't they teach us to think?" When I asked them to describe their dreams, all I got were blank or embarrassed looks. They didn't seem to have any. "What a weird question: dreams? We dream of landing a job and earning a living, that's all."

I remember a handsome young boy with alert, intelligent eyes, who was convinced that he and his fellow high school students had no status in society; nothing they said could change anything. No one would listen to them. It wasn't even worth thinking about. "It's hopeless."

So young and already so fatalistic. What have we done? And these young people lived in a democratic country, very pleasant compared to many others, and with a high standard of living. I was stunned.

Several students were only interested in learning what was immediately useful. "Why study math? I want to be a writer,"

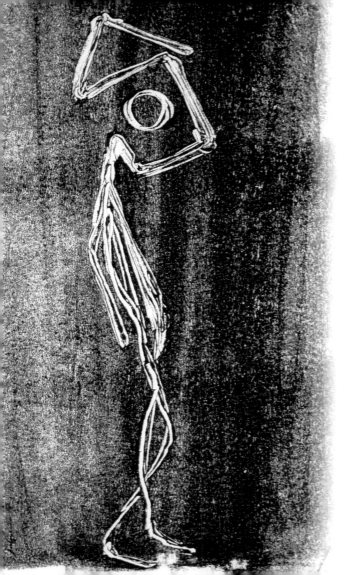

one student said. "All I need are language and literature courses." Another told me: "Who needs the humanities; I want to be an engineer." They wanted to be taught only what they needed in order to earn money. Above all, they didn't want to waste time. Talk about a business culture!

Their comments astonished me, but they seemed equally surprised that anyone would bother to ask them what they thought. Several told me they were not used to being consulted this way.

On top of this, some teachers told me they didn't even have enough time to teach the curriculum set by the Ministry of Education, and they were left with no time at all to talk and exchange ideas with their students.

Others pointed out teachers these days have to compete with video games and television.

Young people "zap" you very quickly. They're not used to concentrating for any length of time on a complex subject.

Increasingly, information is made visual and scripted by the media. On the other hand, young people have a more global view, thanks to the increased access to information and communication with people in foreign lands.

What surprised me the most was the response to the question: What are the qualities of the ideal teacher? Some students answered: a teacher who smiles, who greets you in the morning and is passionate about his or her subject; an enthusiastic teacher. When I asked teachers for their vision of an ideal student, they replied: a young person who comes to school smiling and wants to learn, is enthusiastic. I found this amusing. I've heard the same comment so often in companies, whether in France or in North America. Yet a smile costs nothing. It's simple. It's available to all. Listening to them all, I thought we should undertake a collective intelligence program in a school district. No wonder it's difficult to get adults to smile when they already stopped smiling back in school.

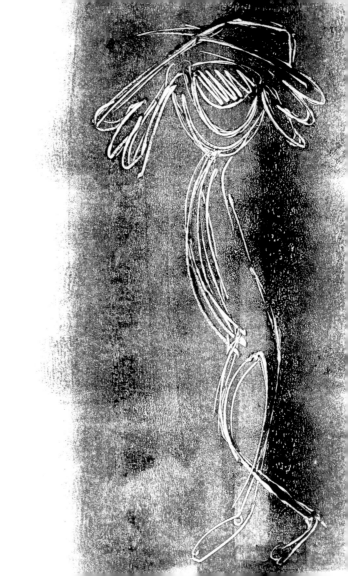

Unfortunately, school structures are a little too heavy and bureaucratic to experiment with pilot projects. Programs in public schools are relatively rigid, compared to those in alternative schools. Having said this, according to teachers, educational reforms now being introduced should improve the situation. Let's hope so, because the need is pressing.

Between viewing video clips, I went walking on Ste. Helene's Island, on the Saint Lawrence River. I thought of Socrates, and how we're drifting further and further away from his teachings.

School should be a place of reflection and ongoing dialogue about ideas, society and the importance, not just of success, but living one's life successfully. School should be more than a place for transmitting knowledge, because that's something the student can always find elsewhere, whether on the Internet, in books or at home. School should primarily be a place to transmit values — that's the essence of education. It should be a place to experiment, and to live these values on a daily basis. Every student should feel responsible for their education. It's a co-construction they are building along with their teachers and parents. They should also feel responsible toward the society that they will help build. That in itself would constitute a first step toward citizenship.

I thought of Theodore Zeldin, a contemporary thinker and professor at Oxford, who suggests we should conduct a conversation on three levels — emotional, intellectual and cultural — to resolve our social and organizational problems. "We work in jobs that demand no more than twenty to twenty-five per cent of our potential."[3] It begins at school. If we get in the habit of functioning below our potential, we kill our desires and add to the cynicism around us.

"This century's biggest mistake," Zeldin says, "was that we accepted boring jobs in exchange for more exciting leisure time. We shouldn't split our private and professional lives." It provides little hope to young people and diminishes their appetite for the future.

At work too, shouldn't we be making our dreams come true by developing our abilities, by creating a stimulating environment?

Knowledge, really, is learning how to learn. Only students can be producers of knowledge. Teachers can help them to give meaning to this knowledge, they can accompany them in the experience, but their primary role is to stimulate the desire to learn.

How can we give young people this drive toward greater heights, this desire to rise up to aim for exceptionality rather than banality? Isn't this what Nietzsche really meant when he repeatedly argued, "The goal is not 'humanity,' but rather the 'superhuman'!"[4]

How can we encourage teachers to teach in this way, and how can we contribute to this type of learning? How do we give children a taste for tomorrow?

"Without you, without the affectionate hand you extended to the small poor child that I was, without your teaching and example, none of this would have happened to me. I don't make a great fuss over this sort of honor (prize for his novel *The First Man*). But at least it gives me the opportunity to tell you what you were and remain to me, and to assure

you that your efforts, your work and the generous heart you put into it are still alive in one of your little pupils who, despite his age, has never ceased to be your grateful student."

Albert Camus to Germain Louis, his teacher in Algiers

By the time I'd returned from my long walk by the river in the brisk and refreshing air, I'd made up my mind. My thoughts alone were not worth much, but if I managed to convince the school commissioners to become more passionately involved, something might change. I decided to talk to them.

Because I've always believed, as Boris Cyrulnik puts it so well in *The Ugly Little Ducklings*, that "the world changes as soon as we speak, and we can change the world by speaking,"[5] I decided to speak frankly with them.

However, as the subsequent evaluation showed, the truth is not always easy to bear. Some commissioners wanted to shoot the messenger. My appearance before this group was appreciated by only a few, by some of the younger ones, I think.

I should mention that more than half the commissioners were scheduled to retire shortly. And I had the feeling that some just didn't feel concerned.

It's also true that the hour was late and, after a day of golf and a few drinks with their meal, my hosts may have felt that my slightly dramatic reflections on the future of young people, school and society, and especially on the responsibility that falls on all our shoulders, were not that easy to digest.

We're living in a time when victims are treated as heroes. It's increasingly difficult to incite people to heroic acts. My call didn't inspire a desire to act as I'd hoped. What I was asking seemed to them too difficult to achieve. I saw little evidence there of the vocation of "transmitter" of knowledge and values.

In hindsight, I came to see that the vision I presented of the situation was not just mine, but also that of many young people, teachers and school principals who were worried about the future.

It was a critical view, reflecting a crucial reality. Difficult, but crucial.

Luckily I'd warned the organizers that I don't always get unanimous approval. My ideas often upset people. This was one of those occasions.

Coming out of the building where my talk had been held, I felt a warm, fine rain on my face. The short walk back to my hotel helped to relax what remained of my tension. Such experiences necessarily create self-doubt. If it hadn't been for some of the responses from young people, I would feel I was battling too much against the current to keep going.

Would I do better to keep quiet? What was I looking for, exactly? Problems? Why was I so stubborn? Where did this passion for change come from? I was happy to have a night ahead me. I reminded myself: "Sleep and dreams provide good counsel."

In the morning, with my first sip of coffee, I recalled Edgar Morin's words. "Humanity is rich in complementarities, which we too often tend to reduce to antagonisms." I certainly didn't want to fall into Manichean thinking, where one side is right and the other is wrong.

This sort of opposition is not useful. We have to create links and think of our common destiny as a society, not only from a national point of view, but also from a global perspective.

One of the greatest successes of education in Quebec is, without question, its international program. Students who've been lucky enough to take part in it demonstrate a degree of curiosity, intellectual alertness and culture that are a pleasure to hear and see.

It is one of the public school system's greatest achievements. Of course I told the commissioners this. But some commented: "We can't very well transform every class into an international program." Another said: "She gave too many foreign examples; we would have preferred to hear examples from Quebec." This last attitude really surprised me, because you would think that people would want to hear about and be inspired by things they don't know rather than hearing the same old examples again and again.

I was also struck by the parallel between those young people in the regular curriculum, who demonstrated little interest in the welfare of others, and the school commissioners who didn't seem to appreciate the window on the world I was offering. I admit I was disappointed to find this attitude among those in the field of education.

The international studies program was developed after the Second World War in the hope that such wars and atrocities would not be repeated. The program, which aims to teach tolerance and an openness toward others, seems to have had excellent results. The young people I met in the program had a desire to share with and help others; I was very moved by them, and by their curiosity about all things.

It made me think about the selection process that puts people in positions of power in any given field. It seems to me that it's not enough to have a degree in administration. I think it's time we put the humanities back in fashion.

The only thing that can really unite us is to share the same values, to share a common dream. Without this basic element, it will be difficult to build anything at all together.

One of the conditions for the success of any project is vision, as I said in the preceding chapter. But we also need reciprocal understanding of certain core values, of which respect is the most important.

A brief anecdote on the subject of respect: the day after my keynote talk, we began our seminar. In spite of a reminder from the facilitator at the start of the first session, a cell phone started ringing five minutes into the workshop. Five minutes later, another phone rang. And then a third.

I couldn't help asking them how they expected students to respect their teachers in class when they didn't respect each other. My comment angered some, to the point that they left the room and didn't return. Despite their age, I felt I had to say something. With young people, one must absolutely lead by example. If there's a lack of openness and respect at the top, how can we demand anything different from the young?

If, as we age, we lose our sense of solidarity with the society in which we live, why should young people feel any solidarity with us?

I was reminded of the students in their last year of high school who had shown no interest in improving the school. Those coming up behind would just have to manage, as they had. When you hear such things from the mouths of graduating students who have spent their last few years in a school, you lose hope in the possibility of building a learning and supportive society.

The organizers of the seminar, and a few of the commissioners, mostly the younger ones (in other words, the next generation of leaders) seemed motivated and truly ready to think about the future and experiment with new approaches to improve the situation. As for the others, I had the impression that any reconsideration of the status quo was unthinkable. They projected an image of self-satisfaction, and seemed to hope for as little disruption as possible while they awaited retirement.

Once again, I had an example of how those in power, privileged by the system, have difficulty sharing power and calling themselves into question. And as soon as the powerful start putting the brakes on, there's little hope of achieving the other conditions necessary for a project's success.

For a project to succeed, we have to create links, to include everyone, and to let everyone share in the results of our collective effort. We must accompany others rather than direct them, seek engagement rather than mere execution. Delegation is important, but without losing interest: we have to follow up closely.

Finally, we have to learn to think for ourselves and help others grow and evolve. To accomplish just that much requires a great deal of humility and generosity.

As Edgar Morin says: "We are always in danger of being wrong, of being deluded. Today, the main mental danger is having a reductive view of the human being. In education, the disciplines are cut off from each other; one deals with Homo Sapiens, the other with Homo Faber, or Homo Economicus… This pigeonholing method of thinking has made us lose the ability to link various areas of knowledge, to situate them in their context, to treat them as a whole."[6]

And yet the human being is a whole, global being, whose behavior would perhaps be more coherent if we put more importance on interdisciplinarity.

Patrick A. Duignan and Narottam Bhindi's study published in the *Journal of Educational Administration*[7] shows that student success rates are higher when an atmosphere of benevolence prevails in the classroom, when students feel respected and trusted, and when there is a good rapport between teachers and other school personnel. **We are influenced by our surroundings.**

"There are no dreams and no desires except in transformation, in the human being's adjustments to the movement of possibility. We all oscillate constantly between love and hate, euphoria and depression, enthusiasm and indifference, sympathy and antipathy, attraction and repulsion, positive and negative, good and bad, etc.," explains Saverio Tomasella. "Human beings are fundamentally imperfect because they are always in a state of becoming."[8]

School is fundamentally imperfect because it is always becoming. My criticisms are not stones idly cast, but rather a reflection on what we might do differently.

It's sometimes easier to examine and judge another generation than it is to look at our own. Yet my experience played the role of a mirror for me: looking at these young people, I saw my own generation under a magnifying glass.

Leadership is a relationship between those who aspire to lead and those who accept to follow. Without the confidence of others, no one can develop their leadership. Each of us must choose to lead or follow according to certain values.

"The meaning of the human adventure," as Edgar Morin puts it, "is not yet decided."[9] Let's get involved in that decision, while there's still time.

The site of the school board conference was pleasant, facing a lake, just outside the city of Montreal. The organizers did a remarkable job, and I still feel slightly uncomfortable at having caused such a stir.

ASTONISHMENT

I owe them this book. Between the title of the video I showed that day, *Young People Without Desires*, and my wish to tell young people we were listening to them, the desire to write *School of Desires* sprung up very naturally. I'm trying to write today what I was unable to say to them at the time.

I know that some of them are already trying to transform the dream into reality. There is hope. But despite their passion and altruism, they need our encouragement to continue their work. We can't remain indifferent to their efforts. Their acts do count for something. The teachers, personnel, administrators and school principals devoted to the cause are more heroic than we think, because they go against the current of the prevailing "Why should I care?"

As for the young people, I heard their call for help. This book is proof of that. I hope there will be many more of us to stand up and be counted.

Vaudreuil, Quebec, May 2002

ASTONISHMENT

"Beauty, it's everywhere you lay your eyes."

Eric-Emmanuel Schmitt

*Mr. Ibrahim and the Flowers of the Koran*

7

It dawned on me that over half my life was already behind me. Suddenly I realized that the closer I am to death, the more I like to stop and listen to silence. My relationship with time is changing. It stretches. The slowness of a single minute's passage is precious to me. Such moments etch themselves more deeply in my memory than do those of earth-shaking events. I'm astonished by this realization. Is this what getting old is?

Before I knew it the month of May was gone. Apart from the blossoming trees that I saw suddenly as I turned a corner on one of my walks, no one had alerted me of summer's approach. If someone had, I hadn't heard them. I was so preoccupied with my own stress that I was oblivious to the beauty around me. In the spring, nature's awakening is swift; you have to open your eyes or miss those luminous, almost transparent greens that last only a few days. It's the awakening of beauty that knows it has but a few months to live.

I rose early and went to bed late. In between, time flew by, and the shadows darkened below my eyes. The demands on me intertwined like colored threads on a loom. I was living at high speed, and felt like an old road warrior with no hope of a different life. Yet now, a small voice in the back of my mind kept asking: "Is this really the life you want? If not, wake up before it's too late." It was as though my daydreams were trying to wake me up.

My field is communications. My first encounter with that word sparked a lasting passion; as though I'd been struck by lightning. I was 20 years old. Until then I'd been looking for something that might interest me, toying with the idea of studying law. One summer's internship was enough to convince me that law wasn't for me. When I discovered communications in university, I knew I'd found my path. Finding one's path is like falling in love. I had suddenly sprouted wings.

For years I rose every morning at 4 o'clock to study. I worked during the day, and went to school at night to take courses or teach. I loved it. I was bitten by the bug. Everything remotely linked to communications interested me.

I remember people asking me if I was bionic, juggling a thousand projects at once: doing research, writing an article, reviewing a book, working on a corporate project. I was a whirlwind, and made my friends' heads spin. I knew there was potential in me, as there is in every one of us. I wanted to discover it through study and action. All at once.

While some wondered what bug had bitten me, I just wanted it to keep on biting. "Energy is a gift," I was told. But isn't it also the effect of a drug called passion?

Already at that time, I felt the desire to be in harmony with the world. For me, my personal evolution was intricately linked with that of my society; I had to read and study hard to better understand and help. I was inhabited by an inexplicable sense of urgency, as though communications was a new miracle cure that only needed to be fine-tuned.

I'd turned all the facets of my life into small laboratories. In my notebook, each successful experience boosted the tally of my ideals. Every failed experience went on the blacklist of lost illusions.

But I wasn't discouraged easily. Difficulties only fanned the flames of my passion. No one said it was going to be easy. I was ready for the fight. Whenever I fell, I was on my feet in a flash. Those were the years when the fighter in me was born. No one could have predicted such strength and determination in the gentle, dreamy child I'd been.

A flame had been lit and I was ablaze. Unstoppable. If the clock could be turned back and the same situation recreated, but without the feeling of urgency, I'm sure my energy would quickly evaporate.

My passion for communications lasted ten years. After that, a series of disappointments made me realize that I had set my ideals very high. I was still convinced that human beings, given certain conditions, could become better people, but I'd also learned, painfully, that they could disappoint.

I had great difficulty, and still do, in accepting these lessons about the darker side of humanity. Wisdom is not given to everyone. To achieve it, I have to work at it, every day.

At the age of 30, the most revealing (and upsetting) realization to come out of my experiences was that there is a dichotomy between discourse and reality. People said one thing, then did the opposite.

Senior managers preached convincingly in press conferences, in general meetings or in front of their employees, but when we were *in situ*, it was another story. I can imagine you smiling as you read these lines: "Things haven't changed much," you're thinking. I know. Alas!

Out of this realization, or rather this frustration, another desire was born in me: to build my own small company, to be free to choose clients with whom I could share the same values, the same beliefs. I would take on clients who would allow me to innovate and continue my experiments, always trying to foster a few dreams at the end of the day.

By chance, during my thirties, that's what happened. There were exceptional men like Michel Kazeef, wonderful clients of whom I won't speak here, having written about them in *City of Intelligences*. Thanks to their trust, I was able to develop the collective intelligence approach.

They offered me their companies as a place to experiment and their employees as colleagues.

Ten fascinating years followed. And we were able to prove the value of my basic premises.

Now, six years further down the road, I see things have regressed. In only a few years, the trio of power, profit and speed has won over in more than a few cases. Hence my doubts. And my desire not to continue in the same way.

Have I become more critical? Or just grown older? Both, really. Have they changed? Some are gone; others are still there. Some have been bitten by the bug of power and a hypertrophy of ego; others have resisted, remained humble, open and generous. I must admit, however, that the latter are few.

**We are influenced by our surroundings** and, if we're not careful, we can easily be swept along by the current of privilege and power. By fashion and trends. By speed and brutalization of the spirit.

Nicole, a friend of mine, has suggested a lovely image to express this: "It's as though you were driving at 100 miles an hour on the freeway, telling yourself that you'd like to turn around, but you can't because you're going too fast." Before you can turn, you have to slow down.

Having said this, I like that little voice that scolds me from inside. I would worry if I no longer heard it.

I'd like to think it's my heart warning my head not to do too many foolish things in my life.

To live your life based on a non-desire is not really living. Admitting this is the first step in the search for a new life.

Quebec writer Michel Dorais has said: "Without frustration, no desire; without desire, no frustration. You can't have one without the other. Which is why we must learn to deal as well with one as with the other. To achieve such wisdom is not easy, I admit. The search for the right balance between desires and frustrations is a lifelong challenge."[1]

I wanted to melt the snow on my wings,
abandon the dogma of reasoning that's too sure of itself.
I wanted to be swept away by places that set the head spinning,
where beauty is no longer a commercial ornament imposed on
the masses, but the purity of what remains as yet untouched.

At the age of 40, I became conscious of the hold marketing has on our lives. Twenty years ago, it seems to me, we were far more critical. We might have let ourselves be manipulated, but we were more conscious of it. We denounced propaganda wherever we saw it. It angered us.

Today, I'm not sure we even ask the question. We seem too willing to go along. So willing that, one day, it became clear to me that I could no longer practice public affairs as I had in the past. Don't misunderstand me; I have always maintained a high ethical standard. In my soul and in my conscience.

The day I began to doubt myself, I quit. It was a question of intellectual honesty. I can only defend causes I believe in. I won't play the puppet or prop girl for a small circle of enormously powerful people who abuse their position.

Before I agree to represent clients, I have to be sure of their intentions. But, with the spread of rampant capitalism and the monopolization of certain sectors, it has become increasingly difficult to gauge people's true intentions.

At first, none of this was really clear to me. I felt uncomfortable, but I didn't know why. I could see that management decisions seemed more and more wrong-headed, or that they came from too far away. In fact, they came from so far away that people affected by them had no real say in them at all.

I felt that they wanted toadying yes-men to create manipulative discourses, rather than advisers with integrity. Shameless manipulation had become acceptable. No one said so, but that's how it felt.

It was all a bit like the period of the war in Iraq. If you felt something had gone awry with respect, democracy, openness and honesty, you will know what I mean. The discomfort I felt was very similar.

I think public opinion was once more demanding, more uncompromising. When something unacceptable was done, and we realized we were being manipulated, we reacted.

I knew I had to write this book, if only to see more clearly. I also owed an explanation to the readers of *City of Intelligences*, because things have changed since 1998. But I hesitated; I didn't feel like rehashing all these issues. I was afraid it would make depressing reading. I couldn't begin until I had decided to write about desire and beauty and, especially, to write for young people.

I had a pressing need to rediscover the marvelous in my life. I had to rekindle my flame. I had no idea how, but the desire was there. At least, there was that.

I chose the form of a memoir because my story is intimate and speaks for no one but me.

I'll let the experts denounce the international political and economic situation. I only want to bear witness, and to find, at the end, hope and a path of action. Yet if we don't know where we've come from, it's hard to know where we're headed.

When *City of Intelligences* appeared in 1998, I declined to join up with an American publishing and speakers network. Product marketing strategies seemed in contradiction with the content of my book. I had the feeling that they wanted to turn me into a guru. I was even asked to join a movement linking companies (a collective work project) to spirituality (an intimate and personal space we have no right to impinge upon). It was going to pay millions. It repulsed me. Of course, I said no.

Everything has become fodder for the market. It was as if they were putting me on the market like a product. It was the very antithesis of the creative approach for which I argue in my book.

One year later, in 1999, I was in a meeting with publishers in Paris when one of them explained that, for him, selling a book was no different than selling canned peas. If I wanted to break into the French market, I would have to agree to his proposed promotional campaign, without hesitation, including interviews that seemed to have nothing to do with the book.

I was disconcerted, because I wanted the book to gently make its way in the world. It had not been conceived for the barrage of advertising he was proposing. Everything was already in the book; I had nothing more to say.

In the end, thanks to my friend Marielle Bloch-Dollande, chair of Beauvais International — a CEO who is open to new approaches and applies them brilliantly in her own company — I was lucky to sign with another publisher, a professional with integrity who was much admired, Geoffrey Staines, founder of Village Mondial Publishers, which has since been bought by Pearson Education.

I'd found an editor who would not impose the canned peas strategy. Thanks again, Marielle.

We create stars in every domain. The danger is to become duped by our own so-called success. Were we chosen because we're offering something thoughtful and original, of value and weight? Not always. Most of the time, we're chosen because someone thinks they can reap big sales.

Which doesn't mean that everything that sells well is no good. Rarely are that many people wrong. On the other hand, when success is too calculated, I find it less interesting. I'm more pleased when a small publisher has a sudden success with one of their authors, and they can hardly keep up with the demand for the book. It's reassuring to see that we can still be surprised, that big successes are not just fabricated in the halls of the powerful or the result of clever marketing strategies.

We should beware of the trio: power-profit-speed. In Stéphane Duperray and Raphaële Vidaling's book, *Cover —Front Pages of the Century*, they map out the gradual slide of the last few years. In the past, magazine cover stories gave artists an opportunity to create works and gave readers some insight into art, but today cover stories tend to try simply to answer the perennial marketing question: "What's going to sell?"

We put beauty at risk when we let ourselves be swept up in what the masses want. Taste must be nourished, like sight. The more we travel, the more open we become.

The more we discover, the more our tastes broaden. The opposite is equally true. The more we allow marketing and profits to govern our lives, the more our vision narrows and our taste is restrained to what is already seen, already known.

My experiences during that period provided much food for thought on this issue. André Deblois, with whom I had worked very pleasurably several years earlier at the time of my multimedia conference *A Future to Invent*, had asked me to give two talks for the Entrepreneurship Foundation in Quebec City and in Montreal.

Considering my packed schedule, I should have turned him down, but André was very persuasive. I knew he was a true professional and I could count on him, so that the contract wouldn't take up too much of my time. As expected, the talks went smoothly.

The organizing team is one of the best I know in Quebec, and feedback from both organizers and participants was very positive. Everyone was satisfied. I didn't regret my involvement.

But during my preparations I had doubts. My career as a speaker is quite accidental; I much prefer to work behind the scenes. But in the past five years, I have often been thrust into the spotlight, even if I didn't intend it that way.

I don't accept many such engagements, and carefully consider each invitation, accepting only those I know will bring me pleasure as well.

As I prepare, I ask myself many questions. I integrate feedback I've received in the past, and try to create a balance, meeting peoples' expectations while providing a few surprises. My real pleasure is in creation, and the interventions I prefer are the risky ones. I see them as co-creations with the audience. It's a little reckless, I admit, but very stimulating. For a person who doesn't particularly enjoy public speaking, you might say I do it on purpose. I dive in with butterflies in my stomach.

"Anguish," Michel Dorais tells us, "goes hand in hand with desire. Our traumas are never more present than when we attempt to surpass them."[2]

I sometimes feel uncomfortable as well with the promotion of events, aimed at attracting an audience. I don't like the idea of being compared to other speakers. It makes me feel like a soap brand, with tags like "among the best…, You've heard X, now here's Y…" At the same time, I understand that organizers have to fill the seats and make the event profitable.

It always comes back to the old "What sells?"

Not being associated with a university, I rely on my speakers' fees to continue my research and to write. I've no intention of biting the hand that feeds me.

I'm simply looking for some middle ground. My solution is to do nothing in particular, to let things come as they may and follow my intuition, knowing that I'm bound to make mistakes.

I accept this, as long as I learn some new lesson each time.

When I start to feel too passive in my marketing strategy, I recall Marguerite Yourcenar's phrase: "Immobility itself, wherever it reigned, was composed of hundreds of dynamisms in balance with each other."[3]

**Astonishment**

I know that life's intelligence will do what's best.
I let things come.

By always weighing, measuring and evaluating, don't we risk turning ourselves into a finished product, completely uniform, with no flaws and no soul? Wouldn't it be sad to become as dull as the covers of magazines?

Feedback from my talks has taught me the importance of taking risks, of allowing some disorder; it's taught me the beauty of imperfection, the unfinished. The anti-formula. The success that surprises. The unexpected moment that moves us.

Students in Quebec's universities are asked to evaluate their professors. I wonder if that doesn't end up bringing the level down to the lowest common denominator. To get a good evaluation, teachers don't dare hand out bad grades, criticize or demand too much from their students. They become what their students expect of them in order to get a passing grade.

To get others to like you. To seduce. How can we avoid this all too human trap? Isn't our human quest, rather, a step-by-step movement through a mystery whose beauty is revealed only gradually, and is dependent on the angle of our gaze, the attitude of our heart and the risks we are willing to take?

A seduction in which our imagination does the stripping is always more seductive than the kind that shows everything, leaving no room for our dreams or fantasies.

But new ideas tend to trouble people. They are inevitably misunderstood. Maybe we have to learn to accept that we can't understand everything right away, by applying our usual criteria. Why not give ourselves time to discover.

Nina Berberova offers a fine example of this in one of her novels, speaking of the Jewish journalist Uria Kovner: "Kovner represents our entire era, all of us, two generations coming thirty to fifty years after his death. Dostoevski was shocked by him exactly as Schiller would have been shocked by the story of the chamber pot in *The Eternal Husband*. Kovner probably shocked other people, but for me, it's significant that he shocked this genius who had such a powerful premonition of the future, and has been so necessary, so essential to that future. But this genius did not realize that we were already there, that the 20th century had arrived in the 19th! Here was the new man in person, precursor, herald (as yet inactive) of millions of men to come. His style, his character, his personality, his destiny, everything that was essential and typical about him went unrecognized: a significant error on the part of his time!"[4]

It's a mistake probably made in every era, but perhaps more so in our own, because we seek to package everything: personalities, styles, looks, talents, success. Increasingly fashion has replaced art. We ought to be forewarned.

When I was young I often wanted others to think well of me. One day I hope I'll be wiser, and place less importance on the judgment of others. Life has been generous, even if I've had my share of criticism. At the moment, it hurts. It's an unexpected blow. But, with time, it helps you to gain some perspective. And even to begin again. To dare again.

In a world that had faith in beauty, we would encourage these attempts at creativity and be careful not to judge others too rapidly. Otherwise, those who are more sensitive might keep quiet and we'd never benefit from their creations.

I'm thinking in particular of young people, of those artists-in-the-raw who have neither the networks nor the money necessary to gain recognition. These young artists may have neither the temperament nor the desire to become another prefabricated product.

We ought to open our doors to them, allow them to exhibit their work and express themselves. Those who are quick to put down whatever surprises them or is unfamiliar should restrain their comments.

Constructive criticism can help one grow, but gratuitous criticism can cause irreparable damage. Our identity is constructed in dialogue with those we love.

Authenticity, that beautiful quality, is born of our human relations. In a society that measures too much, human beings risk becoming more and more like robots whose every move and word is calculated for effect.

If we encourage only success based on a single model, we shouldn't be surprised to find we've built an increasingly banal and uniform society that kills creativity instead of encouraging it.

What I fear most about this obsession with measuring value in accordance with "what sells" is that we allow ourselves to be put to sleep by superlatives, seeking only what shines on the surface. The glitter.

What a sad society it would be that only had room for a few prefabricated heroes, and none for others to fulfill themselves.

We might do better to recreate the atmosphere of the drawing rooms and academies of the 17th and 18th centuries.

In those places, great minds gathered to share poetry, equations and theories, with spirit and freedom. We were a long way then from the desire to package everything according to ready-to-think recipes. In his work "Cross-fertilization, Mind-rubbing, Think Tank, etc.," Gore Vidal talks of intellectual greenhouses where the friction between minds gives birth to sparks called revolutions, inventions or cultural upheavals. "It has been proven that these social microcosms, when they operate intelligently and in harmony, can surpass the isolated individual."

It's our responsibility to create such a crucible of feeling so as to broaden our visions and our lives, and to realize how important we are to one another.

Montreal, June 2002

FIXED IDEA

"The actualization of a fixed idea often cures us of that idea.
But, though we may be cured of the idea,
we are never cured of its cause."

Yukio Mishima

*Thirst for Love*

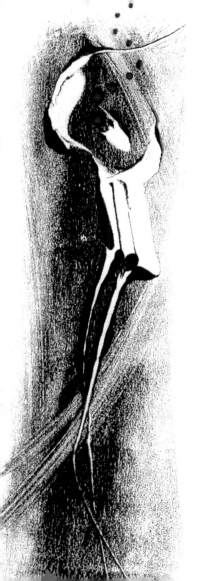

8

Two seminars, one after the other, with little rest between — that's what awaited me in Paris. Even though my life had been moving at breakneck speed the last few months, crossing the Atlantic in either direction always did me a world of good. It was as though I'd put drops in my eyes. My sight became slightly foggy during the trip. I had my own way of moving, almost in a dream-state, thanks to my familiarity with the journey.

As soon as I left the airport, my lethargy fell away, and I looked at the city with eyes that were at once both new and full of memories. I loved the semi-euphoric, semi-nostalgic atmosphere created by this game which, by then, had become a ritual involving my gaze, my imagination and my memory.

I was always happy to be back in my Paris neighborhood. I felt at home there. Three years earlier, when I'd first moved in, I'd been quickly made to feel welcome.

Was it my "slightly sing-song accent," as they called it, or my smile? I'll never know, but the human warmth offered by my neighbors had made my new life so much easier. As a foreigner alone in Paris, I was grateful for their kindness.

Since the end of the summer of 2001, I had spent no more than a few days a month there, because of a contract in North America. As soon as I returned, I'd go round for the latest news from the owners of Pressing d'Artois and other merchants where I did my shopping. I'd stop for a bite, either at the Italian restaurant or at the corner bistro. It was all very pleasant. I knew that when I moved, I would miss all these people. In a short time, we'd built up a complicity through the daily exchange of smiles and little jokes.

I liked to watch the elderly people who always ate lunch in the same places. They were treated like royalty. What I saw there was a lovely way to grow old in your own neighborhood. I think it's infinitely better than being confined to a retirement home. In America, elderly people tend to congregate more in the big shopping malls. At my hairdresser's, they always made a fuss over one elderly client, who was still beautiful and very feminine. All the regulars were fast friends with Françoise the colorist and Roselyne the esthetician. I enjoyed the familiarity and warm atmosphere of that small neighborhood salon. Even if it was only a short walk from the Élysée Palace, it was unpretentious.

It's true that as soon as I arrived in Paris, I developed a surprisingly affectionate attitude. There was a kind of poetry in all my encounters, in everything I saw and experienced. At first, everything seemed magical.

Doors opened effortlessly; a network formed naturally. I felt as though I had come at just the right moment. In hindsight, I can't be sure I didn't imagine it all. There was so much that was unreal in my Parisian adventure. I'm just happy to have garnered such beautiful memories. It was nothing grandiose, just small joyful moments (which is already a lot).

But what is most precious to me is the friendship of a few extraordinary people. As we grow older, it's more difficult to make new friends with whom we feel we can share everything. For me, France really was a land of welcome. There I found the kind of friendships that one rarely finds in a lifetime.

As a result, returning to Paris was always a celebration. My only regret was that I didn't have time to see every one of my friends.

My work too was a pleasure. My clients, all hand-picked, were those with whom I felt complicit. I'm unable to work with a client for very long unless we share the same values. I need that complicity. It's absolutely vital.

**Fixed Idea**

It was warm and sunny. The sun rose early and set late. It made you want to be outdoors as much as possible. Luckily, we'd chosen a houseboat moored on the Quai d'Orsay to hold our seminars. Evenings and mornings, I crossed the Place de la Concorde, walking along the Seine in a different light. The sky, the trees, the architecture: everything was so beautiful and harmonious, I realized how much I needed this beauty in my life at that moment.

I was apprehensive about the seminar, because all the participants were men. I prefer diversity; it's better for creativity. And women — when they aren't hiding behind the mask of power-hungry warrior, or seducer willing to do whatever it takes to succeed or attract attention — bring a touch of authenticity and emotion that lifts the men to another level. A more sincere register, more empathetic. When it happens, it's the quintessence of leadership in the feminine.

This time the men were exceptional: committed, listening, authentic and creative. I won't soon forget them. Very quickly they established an extraordinary complicity. It was beautiful to watch these beings full of sensitivity and intelligence. The dynamism of these ten managers and the positive effect it was bound to have once they returned to their teams was, in my opinion, priceless. The passion elicited by a collective intelligence approach is a confirmation of its usefulness.

During each of my monthly stops in Paris, the senior management team would meet at my apartment. It had become a Thursday evening ritual. They had a front row seat to follow the progress of our project. For a while, with these accomplices, I really thought we could change the world. And so did they. It required people with special qualities to opt for such an innovative approach during such conventional times.

They had the courage to question themselves. Plus, they trusted each other and were willing to share their power.

Those working under them for long enough were very grateful to realize this. I say "for long enough," because there were several personnel changes during the project. The composition of the group had changed a great deal, and this affected the results. Alas!

They had to be rigorous. They had to learn to manage the essential: to understand the way processes worked, simplify the methods, and let those doing the work improve them. They had to make the direction clear to everyone, in spite of constant, ongoing changes.

All of this was difficult to do in such a short time and with limited resources. In the field, the younger ones — led by their manager, a young woman full of passion and integrity — became the most enthusiastic ambassadors of the project. You could see their joy and pride at being part of it. It was a project that made people want to grow.

But it wasn't enough to transform a single company.
It was only a microcosm, an island in a sea
under the constant pull of counter-currents.

Big structures are heavy and slow. Their technologies become rapidly obsolete and their processes over-complicated. Companies merge to reduce costs, to increase purchasing power and control salary levels. It's a purely financial rationale, totally disconnected from any human logic. These companies end up centralizing operations and decisions. They do everything but teach their personnel to think and be creative.

Employees spend more time filling in forms and being trained to follow new rules than they do improving the company collectively.

Managing mega-structures becomes, in a way, an abstract job. Leaders no longer feel responsible, and some of them are thinking more about how to make themselves more visible to get another promotion. It seems to me that big companies contribute less and less to developing the intelligence and solidarity of their employees.

There's an "everyone for themselves" mentality that fosters political and careerist behavior. Employees who are less able to behave like this, but seek advancement in the company, are often steered into seminars paid for by the company so as to become more political or, as some put it, more strategic. Unfortunately, the strategies in question are scheming and manipulation.

The many mergers of the last two decades have transformed the economic and organizational landscape. Companies are more and more gigantic. Even unions have gone in the same direction. All these structures become monsters of paralysis where rules and disputes about rules are the order of the day.

Each time one of these mega-structures collapses, the effects are devastating, yet governments no longer really have the power to counter the trend. If they stop a merger at one point in time, the company simply reapplies down the road and eventually gets the green light.

These mega-companies give the impression that they'll stop at nothing to swallow up their competitors and achieve hegemony. The more they think they can do whatever they like, the more they risk collapsing, laying off thousands of people in the process.

It's a financial rationale that benefits a very small number of people. And usually the same people. The truth is that these collapses rarely if ever impoverish those who caused them through bad decisions. Those who do suffer are usually affected several months or years later. The leaders at the origin of the crisis can then shirk their responsibility and put the onus on the economy in general.

The media, for their part, rarely have the time to give us the overall picture which would help us see the links. Closures are in the news one day, and forgotten the next. Or almost.

In spite of all the fiascos, CEOs and management, protected by golden handshakes and generous pensions, are last to be affected. They're the commanders of our modern age. They give the orders, but do not fight. Others are killed in their place, or the children of others.

Having witnessed the evolution of company mergers and the resulting oligarchy from the inside, I'm astonished at how little we react. When I'm feeling depressed, I sometimes sketch out possible scenarios to avoid catastrophes, or ways to reduce their cost to humanity.

My simplest scenario (and, to me, the most effective) relies on us, depends on us. If we stop admiring victims and encouraging our persecutors, there might be fewer victims. Individual awakening: I see no other solution. But for it to work, we would have to wake up all together. Or, at least, it would require a great number of us. The abusers would then realize how difficult it is to go to war without soldiers. Let's replace the psychosis of fear with the desire to build a society founded on solidarity and greater equity.

**The New Powers.** Corporations are becoming our governments. Unions too. They have more and more power. Behind the scenes, they often pull the political strings. But governments that think only of finances and profits for a certain group — a capitalism gone mad, as Joseph Stiglitz, winner of the 2001 Nobel Prize in Economics, calls it — is dangerous for the future of the world. They talk about sustainable development, but how far are they willing to go? In terms of concrete action, their priority is still maintaining the highest possible profits. The word "reasonable" is not really part of their vocabulary.

What's more, in recent years, CEOs and other corporate directors have become used to earning mind-boggling salaries and privileges. Such rapid gains can give them the illusion they're superior to others. They become so self-confident that they no longer take the trouble to consult others before making major decisions.

All this is not always conscious. I see it rather as a gradual slippage linked to how little time they spend reflecting on the consequences of their acts.

That's why it's urgent that corporate personnel, public opinion and the media all wake up and exercise vigilance. Corporate directors must develop a global perspective, paying as much attention to human and environmental concerns as to financial ones. They must think about the long term, beyond the two or three years of their mandates. I'm talking about a real perspective and real convictions, in other words, applied ethics.

We should choose carefully those we intend to follow. The problem is that everything happens so quickly; we live at a rapid pace, and we have so little time to think beyond our immediate tasks. Few people are really aware of the importance of what's at stake, because we have very few tools and time to make the links. The task is difficult, even for those who make the effort.

One thing's certain: we should all feel concerned and take the time to think about it. Sometimes, people wake up too late. I very much appreciated Anne-Lise Grobéty's novel, *The Time of Whispered Words*, the story of two long-time friends, a Jew and a Christian who realize too late they have witnessed the rise of Nazism without reacting. "What I wanted to say," whispered Anton, "what got us into this mess today are those small daily acts of cowardice of which we have all been guilty, for too long… everything we were hearing in the street, in the bistros, the rising anger, the hostility: we let it happen without reacting. We watched hatred and violence give birth to their offspring like bastards, outside our doors, and we were silent…"[1]

"You're right, Anton, we lovers of poetry, of the well-turned phrase, continued to live as though nothing was happening, refusing to see the rottenness that nourished the words in their speeches, and the deadly poison they were spreading around us."[2]

Caught up as we are in our own lives, it's not easy to develop a panoramic view of the world. At work, we would prefer to be liked, not to displease our superiors, not to annoy our colleagues. We need our jobs, and people rarely appreciate someone who is critical. At home, we're exhausted; we may talk more openly with our loved ones, but we try not to get depressed by the way things are. It's a question of survival. Everyone has a right to a bit of peace and happiness. Especially when we spend long hours in a work environment that's not always pleasant.

I may be wrong but, in recent years, I sense that many people just want to shut their eyes. Out of weariness. There's a kind of fatigue in thinking about the fate of the world. The French may have many faults for which we sometimes criticize them, but some of them have the great quality of continuing to think and even daring to say things that go against global commercial thinking. Some even try to act. For all our sakes, we mustn't let them struggle alone.

## Fixed Idea

My personal fixed idea is a desire for an individual and collective awakening. We should react in numbers, each in his or her own way, but toward a common destiny.

How wonderful it would be if this awakening became the fashion, if it swept us up in its wake, exciting and filling us with joy. Rather than seeing it as a denunciation of world hegemony, we should see it as a collective construction. How incredible if a large number of us could be complicit: in business, the media, the arts.

I've named this awakening the *School of Desires*, but we could call it something else. What's important is the idea behind it.

It's my fixed idea. You may have noticed. I'm making it real, bit by bit, through a corporate project here, a seminar there, a book here, a talk there, but the source of the fixation, as Mishima suggests, does not go away. It's an obsession.

I place my belief in the future in us. If only we could determine the future voluntarily. I understand that we can't always be on our guard. We all need an occasional break. But pretending not to see what's going on is no solution either. I'd like to see us venture, once in a while, toward a better world, borrowing the desire that Edwy Plenel attributes to Columbus: "... between habit and adventure he had to choose either to submit to the order of things or to embrace a desire for the world."[3]

What will become of us if we've lost that desire for the world? What will become of us if we turn our eyes away from beauty for too long? Will we still be able to recognize it?

There's still time to wake up. Edgar Morin has a clear view of the current situation: "The planetary era, which began in the 16th century, has in recent years attained the stage we call globalization. In fact, a global civilization is in the making.

Economically and technically, everything is coming into place for a global society. The infrastructure of communications-organization is already in place across the planet, closer and faster than the one required for a large nation-state of fifty years ago. What is lacking are the structures of decision-making, control, law, and the consciousness of a common destiny that characterize a global society, one which goes beyond local societies while preserving them. Although humans have more solidarity, they continue to make enemies amongst themselves, and are capable of unleashing racial, religious or ideological hatred... The planet is like an unfinished spaceship, powered by four engines — science, technology, industry and the economy — but which still lacks a cockpit."[4]

We'll get the pilots we deserve. And the leaders too. If we remain unwilling to get involved, abdicating and not seeing what disturbs us, what then will become of our children and our children's children? If we choose not to react, shouldn't we also do like Georges Brassens and refuse to reproduce? The singer-songwriter decided against having children because he was too worried, too pessimistic about the future of our planet. Of course, life without children is impossible. It would mean an end to all life and any happiness. But since we still choose to give birth to children, we should also build a better world, so that they want to grow up and, in turn, take over the pursuit of beauty.

I wanted my seminars to be moments dedicated to thinking about these questions, to sharing our ideas so as to enlarge our vision of the world, and awaken the desire for a common destiny. I was also hoping there would be magical moments for each participant so that all would get a taste for happiness and be encouraged to transform their dreams into legends, into inspiring stories to tell. I wanted my seminars to give birth to the desire for a different future.

## Fixed Idea

All that was well and fine. It still is. But it's not enough. Hence the idea for this book. To ask for your help by encouraging you to share your ideas and visions, to give you the desire to dream and to act. So as not to leave, as Alessandro Baricco says, the bankers and corporate bosses to create the dream alone in our place. To do so, as we can already see, makes for a rather dreary world.

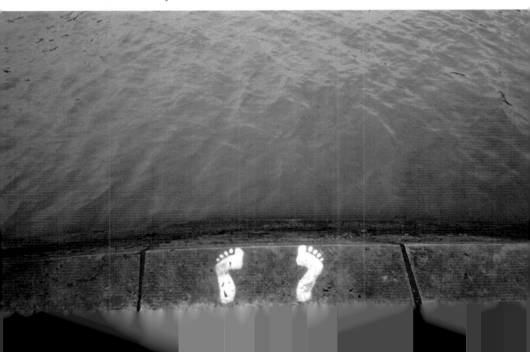

I remember listening to the marvelous poet Christian Bobin tell interviewer Michel Camus about the first thing that marked him as a child. He was three or four years old and, purely on a whim, he admits, he'd called for his parents in the middle of the night. As soon as his mother heard him crying she came, as she always did, and asked him what he wanted. "I don't want you," he replied, "I want Daddy." His loving mother went and woke his father who, in turn, came to the child's bedside to ask him what he wanted. The boy replied that he didn't want anything.

For a long time, Bobin felt that this first memory represented the enigma of a call and will that wanted nothing. Then one day, he spoke of it to someone who made him realize that he'd simply wanted to be reassured that both his parents were there.

He calls and asks for nothing more. Like in his works. He dedicates himself to pulling all things from their slumber until they manifest nothing more nor less than their presence.

## Fixed Idea

"Is anyone there? If someone is there, it must mean I'm here," Bobin adds. It is the need to feel a presence that bears its own truth.

I smiled as I listened to him speak of this child's way of asking questions that call for something else beyond their answer. I smiled because I saw the parallel with this book. A call. And then silence. We'll see what this presence brings.

I smiled because, all through my mother's life, I loved to feel her presence near me. To feel her sitting quietly in the same room. It gave me a feeling of such calm. Even when I was 40 years old and she was 82, I still liked to know she was there, by my side.

Today, it's you I'm calling. You needn't answer, I only want you to show you are present. That's all.

I wanted to make a gesture towards you, so that you, in turn, would make one towards someone else. In this way, we might

form a chain of learning, so as not to let the destiny of our planet slip between our fingers. A call.

But, to be perfectly honest, secretly, I also wanted the alchemy to work on me, so that in the process of writing I would discover new desires, new dreams. In other words, I saw this writing process as a game to elicit the unknown, to spark my imagination. It was my way of teasing fate. A call.

My project was simply to keep an agenda for several months, along with a diary in which I would make the occasional entry, more often than not in airports. The only given I established in advance was to place each chapter in the city where I found myself during its writing. As for the rest, I wanted to surprise myself with what I ended up saying, and with the words of the authors that came to mind along the journey.

As I've already told you, I dive right in with butterflies in my stomach. It's my way to feel alive, and to elicit desire, the only force that can compel me to act. To take action.

More and more, I want to let chance guide my way, so long as I'm in step with my desires. Even if it means occasionally leaping into the dark to provoke it. It's a search for meaning, for desires, for surprises.

"The passage through the undetermined," explains Pierre Faure, "is a phase that frightens us and which we accept to undertake, more often than not, only when constrained by circumstances."[5]

But since there is a desire hidden behind each fear, my only constraint was freedom and the duties it imposes on us and on society.

To kindle in myself the desire for a common destiny, I need to know there's someone out there.

I'll be there if you will.

Paris was in the grip of a heat wave. Breathing was difficult. I decided to escape to the seaside with a friend. We ate a pleasant lunch in Honfleur, and took a long walk on the beach in Trouville.

After seeing them in a movie or a novel, some places make me dream. But when I see some mythical places for real, they disappoint me. I find them beautiful, but tiny and often crowded. Overcrowded.

I'll never understand the dense crowds and their behavior, which is identical from one country to the next, and is often motivated by nothing more than the desire to be crammed together and to make a lot of noise.

I thought how lucky we are in Quebec to still have so many open spaces. I say "still," because we have fewer and fewer of them. And, at the risk of sounding cliché, will we even notice it when — if we're not careful — they disappear for good?

**Fixed Idea**

Let's take the trouble to respect what is still wild, beautiful and pure. Let's not be too cynical or indifferent. Or our Earth itself will pay the price. That's what I told myself that afternoon, as I picked my way among the crowds along the beach.

Empty beaches, quiet places unspoiled by humans, and hours of freedom to enjoy them will be the luxuries of the future.

The following weekend, I went to Giverny, to stroll in Monet's splendid gardens. It was sublime. The flowers were arrayed like queens; I also remember fondly the fields dotted with poppies.

I love my summer strolls in France. Stepping into a 10th century church, walking in narrow twisting streets reserved for pedestrians, enjoying a good meal on a patio in the shade of a one-hundred year old tree, sipping a local rosé wine, I feel as though I were a time-traveler, going back. It reminds me of the importance of protecting everything.

**Fixed Idea**

I was reminded of this at the end of the day when, heading back to Paris, the nightmare caught up to us again: hours of bumper-to-bumper traffic. To think that in 1928, returning to his country home in Lugano, Hermann Hesse had already complained there were too many people on the planet.

When you see the lemming-like behavior of crowds, the tactics of promoters and the attitudes of some people, you have to be pretty stubborn to keep seeing what I do in humanity.

Let's say that, in a crowd, we're not always at our best. But if, from our earliest schooling, we learned a collective intelligence approach, a greater civic sense and less cynicism, who's to say things wouldn't be better a hundred years from now?

Paris, July 2002

to be continued...
Reflections 2

# NOTES

\* indicates translation into English by Majzels and Mouré

## 0 - THE DESIRE FOR DESIRE

1.   Ernesto Sabato, *La Résistance*, Paris: Gallimard, 2000, p. 75.\*

2.   Fernando Pessoa, The Book of Disquiet, trans. Margaret Jull Costa, London: Serpent's Tail, 1991, p. 78.

3.   Saverio Tomasella, "Oser la psychanalyse [To Dare Psychoanalysis]," *Revue Psychanalyse*, #13, June-July 2002. p. 64. \*

4.   Fernando Pessoa , *The Book of Disquiet*, trans. Margaret Jull Costa, London: Serpent's Tail, 1991, p. 141.

5.   Hermann Hesse, "Une leçon d'hygiène artistique [A Lesson in Artistic Hygiene]," in *L'art de l'oisiveté [The Art of Idleness],* Calmann-Levy, 2002, p. 23. \*

6.   Alessandro Baricco, "Next" in *Petit livre sur la globalisation et sur le monde qui vient [Little Book on Globalization and the World to Come],* Albin Michel, 2002, p. 69. \*

7.   Italo Calvino, *Invisible Cities*, trans. William Weaver. New York: Harvest/HBJ, 1978, p. 42.

## 1 - A DISARMING IDEA OF BEAUTY

1. Rainer Maria Rilke, *Sonnets to Orpheus: With Letters to a Young Poet*, trans. Stephen Cohn, NY: Routledge, 2003, p. 194.

2. Jean D'Ormesson, *C'était bien [It was Good],* Paris: Gallimard, 2003, p. 12. *

3. Hermann Hesse, "Gubbio," in *L'art de l'oisiveté [The Art of Idleness],* Calmann-Lévy, 2002, p. 65. *

4. Ernesto Sabato, [La Résistance], Paris: Gallimard, 2000, p. 82. *

5. Ibid, p. 61. *

6. Ibid, p. 108. *

7. François Cheng, *L'éternité n'est pas de trop [Green Mountain, White Cloud],* Albin Michel, 2002, p. 207. *

8. Italo Calvino, *Invisible Cities,* trans. William Weaver. New York: Harvest/HBJ, 1978, p. 82

9. Rainer Maria Rilke, *Sonnets to Orpheus: With Letters to a Young Poet,* trans. Stephen Cohn, NY: Routledge, 2003, p. 177.

## 2 - POWERFUL INFLUENCES

1.  Hermann Hesse, "Gubbio," in *L'art de l'oisiveté [The Art of Idleness],* Calmann-Lévy, 2002, p. 120. *

2.  Erri DeLuca, *Montedidio [God's Mountain],* Paris: Gallimard, 2002, p. 46. *

3.  Cunmin Zhu and Dominique Fernandez, *La Beauté [Beauty],* Desclée de Brouwer, Presses littéraires et artistiques de Shanghai, 2000, p. 7. *

4.  Chateaubriand, *Mémoires d'outre-tombe —1 [Memoirs from Beyond the Grave],* Paris: Gallimard, 1997, p.80. *

5.  Rainer Maria Rilke, *Sonnets to Orpheus: With Letters to a Young Poet,* trans. Stephen Cohn, NY: Routledge, 2003, p. 175.

6.  Anne-Lise Grobéty, *Le temps des mots à voix basse [The Time of Whispered Words],* La joie de lire, Geneva, 2001, p. 64. *

## 3 - FISSURE

1. Fernando Pessoa , *The Book of Disquiet*, trans. Margaret Jull, Costa, London: Serpent's Tail, 1991, p. 41 .*

2. Hermann Hesse, "Pays natal [Native Land]," in *L'art de l'oisiveté [The Art of Idleness],* Calmann-Lévy, 2002, p. 131. *

3. Daniel Bélanger, *Rêver mieux [Better Dreams],* Audiogrammes Records Inc., 2001. *

4. Marguerite Yourcenar, *Auguste Rodin,* La Pléiade, p. 871. *

5. Cyrille J.-D. Javardy and Pierre Faure, Yi Jing, Albin Michel, 2002, p. 26. *

6. Ibid, p. 26. *

7. Noëlle Barbot, "Désirer est un besoin salvateur [Desiring is a Saving Need]", Revue Psychanalyse, #13, June-July 2002.*

8. Ernesto Sabato, [*La Résistance],* Paris: Gallimard, 2000, p. 105. *

## 4 - A PLURAL INTELLIGENCE

1. Marguerite Yourcenar, *Auguste Rodin*, La Pléiade, p. 872. *

2. Rainer Maria Rilke, *Sonnets to Orpheus: With Letters to a Young Poet*, trans. Stephen Cohn, NY: Routledge, 2003, p. 180.

## 5 - EYES WIDE OPEN

1. Cunmin Zhu and Dominique Fernandez, *La Beauté [Beauty],* Desclée de Brouwer, Literary and Artistic Press of Shanghai, 2000, p. 127. *

2. Boris Cyrulnik, *Un merveilleux malheur [A Marvellous Misfortune],* Éditions Odile Jacob, Paris,1999, p. 30. *

3. Caroline Montpetit, 'Gréco l'éternelle aux FrancoFolies [The Eternal Gréco at the Franco-follies]," *Le Devoir*, 19-20 July 2003. *

4. Hermann Hesse, "Légende chinoise [Chinese Legend]," in *L'art de l'oisiveté [The Art of Idleness],* Calmann-Lévy, 2002, p. 240. *

## 6 - LOSS OF ILLUSIONS

1.  François Cheng, *L'éternité n'est pas de trop [Green Mountain, White Cloud],* Albin Michel, 2002, p. 208. *

2.  Boris Cyrulnik, *Les vilains petits canards [The Ugly Little Ducklings],* Éditions Odile Jacob, Paris, 2001, p. 152. *

3.  Theodore Zeldin, *Let's Have a Conversation, Fast Company,* December 2001.

4.  Friedrich Nietzsche, *The Will to Power,* trans. Walter Kaufmann & R. Hollingdale, Vintage Giant, 1968.

5.  Boris Cyrulnik, *Les vilains petits canards [The Ugly Little Ducklings],* Éditions Odile Jacob, 2001, p. 152 *

6.  Tessa Ivascu and Edgar Morin, "Les cinq sens [The Five Senses]", *En vue,* Air France. *

7.  Patrick Duignan and Narottam Bhindi, "Authenticity in Leadership: An Emerging Perspective," in the *Journal of Educational Administration,* vol. 35 no. 3, 1997, MCB University Press, pp. 195-209.

8.  Saverio Tomasella, "Oser la psychanalyse [To Dare Psychoanalysis]," *Revue Psychanalyse,* #13, June-July 2002, p. 63. *

9.  Tessa Ivascu and Edgar Morin, "Les cinq sens [The Five Senses]', *En vue,* Air France. *

## 7 - ASTONISHMENT

1.  Michel Dorais, *La mémoire du désir – Du traumatisme au fantasme [Memory of Desire — from Trauma to Fantasy]*, VLB, Quebec City, 1995, p. 167. *

2.  Ibid, p. 45. *

3.  Marguerite Yourcenar, *Auguste Rodin*, La Pléiade, Paris, 1982, p. 853. *

4.  Nina Berberova, *Le cap des tempêtes [Cape of Storms]*, Actes sud, 2002, p. 70 *

## 8 - FIXED IDEA

1.  Anne-Lise Grobéty, *Le temps des mots à voix basse [The Time of Whispered Words]*, La joie de lire, Geneva, 2001, p. 49. *

2.  Ibid, p. 50. *

3.  Edwy Plenel, *La découverte du monde [The Discovery of the World]*, Éditions Stock, Paris, 2002, p. 117. *

4.  Tessa Ivascu and Edgar Morin, "Les cinq sens [The Five Senses]", *En vue*, Air France. *

5.  Cyrille J.-D. Javardy and Pierre Faure, *Yi Jing*, Albin Michel, 2002, p. 25. *